They all ate and were satisfied, and the disciples picked up twelve basketfuls of broken pieces that were left over.

LUKE 6:21 (NIV)

(There were times when I felt like a leftover, but every piece was important to God!)

KAREN MARRERO

Traitmarker Books

www.traitmarkerbooks.com
traitmarker@gmail.com
Cover Design: Robbie Grayson III

All Scripture references are from the
New International Version (NIV).

Paperback ISBN | 979-8-8690-0440-6

Everyone Needs (Just a Little) Karen

KAREN MARRERO

A PORTRAIT OF **CHILDLIKE FAITH**

The joy of the Lord is your strength.

NEHEMIAH 8:10

To My Husband Santiago—
my best friend who encouraged me
to follow my dreams

To My Sons—
who taught me much about life
and the importance of time together

In Loving Memory of Bryte—
who inspired the title and his stories
live on in this book

To Family and Friends—
for their prayers and encouragement
to write my story

ENDORSEMENTS

"You are beautiful. You are worthy to walk in the destiny that God has called you to walk and minister to hurting women! Your voice will go where others have not reached. You have paid the price."

—Lorraine Swope
1933-2023 | HARRISBURG, PA

"Karen's zany sense of humor captured my interest as I related and connected with the truth principles hidden therein. She shares tough stuff we all face with a dose of comic relief and the reality of God's hope for every situation. I want the first copy of her book!"

—Nancy Sabastian Kuch
Spiritually Single Moms | AUTHOR

Contents

PART IV | *Broken Karen—Divorce*

PART V | *Karen Unchained—Restoration*

A Note
From the Publisher

The publisher is providing this book and its contents on an "as is" basis and makes no representations or warranties of any kind with respect to this book or its contents and disclaims all such representations and warranties, including but not limited to warranties of mental healthcare for a particular purpose.

The content of this book is for informational purposes only and is not intended to diagnose, treat, cure, or prevent any mental condition or disease. This book is not intended as a substitute for consultation with a licensed practitioner. Please consult with a physician or healthcare specialist regarding the suggestions and recommendations made in this book.

Traitmarker Books
Robbie Grayson III | Franklin, TN

A Note
About Names

I altered names to respect the privacy of my sons and other persons. Specifically, I changed the names of my sons in the following ways:

- I changed my firstborn's name to ADAM. Just as Adam in the Bible was the "first man," my firstborn is also the first-born grandson on both sides of the family.
- I changed my secondborn's name to BRYTE. Not only was he business-minded and intelligent with computers, but he was also introspective and intuitive.
- I changed my thirdborn's name to CHASE. He was so unruly as a child, and we sometimes had to chase him down. This pattern continued into his turbulent teen years as I wasn't as informed as I should have been on his whereabouts.

I have also changed the name of my sons' father to Chad so that it will be harder for people to track him down and beat him up!

A Note
About How to Read This Book

Perhaps you know someone named Karen or have encountered an obnoxious Karen (in real life or through various media). Certainly, you have your own opinions. However, this Karen cannot be "put in a box."

Having grown up in a dysfunctional, middle-class family with abysmal communication skills, I survived several years of child sexual abuse that stunted me in more ways than I can count. As a young college student, I married young, perhaps due to my home life. I struggled as a naive mother to raise three sons with varying personalities (two of whom were beyond my ability to parent successfully). All this took a toll on our marriage, which dissolved in its fortieth year. Later, I suffered the death of my second-born son due to the ravages of mental illness.

Finally, I could return to my love of teaching full-time in the challenging surroundings of incarcerated juveniles. I guess some of the challenges I faced with my sons prepared me for this new challenge.

Still, it was the complex combination of these challenging situations that drove this Karen to become an advocate for a demographic I would never have chosen: prisoners, specifically incarcerated juveniles.

So, there are three important points you should keep in mind as you read this book.

First, hard times can be unpredictable. Each of us has different roles in life, requiring us to focus on other things. So when a hardship comes out of nowhere, it can command our focus. That means that the problem gets most or all of our attention.

Second, holding patterns can be disorienting. When a hardship lasts longer than usual, we call it a "holding pattern." A holding pattern can last for weeks, months, or even years. Before we know it, our lifestyles become influenced by hardship. And when the problem finally lets up, we become aware of all the responsibilities, family, and friends we neglected.

Third, God can rescue you from your hardship if you ask Him. Just note that we can't tell him how or when. Just a simple "Help me, LORD" can work!

Despite all of the ways I might have contributed to my problems, God has redeemed me from the abuse of my childhood, the death of my second son, separation and divorce, and so much more. He has helped me forgive myself, develop a better self-image, and build a better life. After three decades of raising my sons and working various jobs, I returned to full-time teaching, had a second chance at love, remarried, and traveled extensively. My social calendar is filled with activities, and my contact list has grown with many friends. It has simply been a miraculous turn of events!

So, while you might think you may have all Karens figured out, I ask you to read my book with an open mind. Because more than learning about one of the many Karens in the world, you might also learn something about yourself.

INTRODUCTION
Just a *Little* Karen

When my middle son was a young teenager, he had a nasty spill while trying out a new bicycle in a store parking lot. Without reporting the incident to the salesperson, he left the bike and promptly returned home. Later on, I found him lounging on the couch watching television, which was unusual behavior—because he didn't like watching television.

"Are you okay?" I asked.

"Well, not really. I fell and hurt my arm." He was blunt but unemotional.

Soon afterward, I was concerned enough to make an appointment with the doctor for X-rays.

"So, how did you hurt yourself?" the nurse casually asked.

"I was test-driving a bike when I fell on the asphalt."

"Oh, how do you spell that? "Never mind—I got it."

Curious, he glanced over her shoulder as she wrote out her diagnosis: *Patient was hurt on ass-fault.*

Without a word, he quietly left (not unlike the bike incident)—but not before he saw that her name tag bore her name in proud caps: KAREN. Later, he shared the story with me and said, "Everyone needs just a little Karen."

It has been over two decades since that visit to the doctor's and twelve years since my son passed, and I've often thought about those prophetic and almost haunting words: *Everyone needs just a little Karen.* It might have seemed nothing more to my son than an uneventful observation, but I cannot help but think that he meant something else or something more and that it was meant for me because my name is Karen, too.

So what are those things? Well, three come to mind.

First, as a career reading specialist, the irony wasn't lost on me that *Karen* and *carin(g)* are homophones: words that sound similar but have different meanings. *Karen* actually comes from the name *Katherine,* which means *pure.* Based on this word association, a Karen has good intentions.

Second, Karen has come to be associated with a woman who has taken on the role of self-appointed protector, defender, and guardian in extreme and sometimes obnoxious ways. So, while a Karen might have good intentions, sometimes (well, a lot of the time!), she can get the essential things wrong (like "ass-fault").

Third, a Karen is just that—a woman named Karen!

What does all this mean for me, and why should

you be interested? Well, another three things come to mind:

First of all, I like to think that my son, in his heart of hearts, spoke these words as a kind of tribute to me: *Everyone needs just a little Karen.* In other words, maybe my son was giving me an underhanded compliment about my contribution to his well-being.

Second, as you will learn in this book, I was a constant presence in not just this son's life but all three. Maybe a little too much. Sometimes, I could have dialed it in or toned it down. Maybe my son was asking me to reign in my "smothering" just a little? That's where *just a little Karen* comes in.

Last, I would like to think that these words betray an affection my middle son had for me but couldn't share with me any other way. And just as he acknowledged that the nurse who couldn't spell "asphalt" correctly was still qualified to diagnose his injury accurately, I would like to think that he also understood that though his mother could not make his pain go away and ultimately could not save him from the harm that would eventually take him from me, he still understood that I was his mother and that I loved him as only a mother could. That's where *Everyone needs* comes in.

So, as a tribute to my middle son, *Everyone Needs Just a Little Karen* is a memoir of my life: a Karen who did the best she could for herself and her family with the little that she had. That is, she had little regard for herself, little knowledge of what a healthy family should be, and little understanding of how these two blunders would shape her and her children's lives. So, *Everyone Needs Just a Little Karen* is my quest to forgive myself for all the blind spots I couldn't see back then but can see now. And my prayer for you is that should you see yourself in any part of my story, you can forgive yourself, too.

And, yes, my middle son did break his arm!

My flesh and my heart may fail,
but God is the strength of my heart.
and my portion forever.

PSALM 73:26 (NIV)

PART I

Little Karen

CHILDHOOD

1

I'm No Artist—
But I'm Drawing Blanks

As a young child, I strongly understood God's love for me. I can't explain it. I just knew in my heart that God loved me.

How did I respond as a child to God's love? I wanted to please Him, so I pleased Him the best way I knew: I obeyed my parents and teachers. That's how I remember my childhood: obeying, being good-natured, and pleasing others.

My brother, Wayne, was my parent's first child. He is about sixteen months older than I am. When he was just a baby, he got pneumonia. Because he was born in August, he probably got sick when it started to get cold. Then he got double pneumonia. Maybe that's why my mom loved him so dearly and kept him close to her. She was so happy he survived.

We were only one grade level apart, so there was a lot of closeness between us. Of course, we had sibling rivalry as we fought for our parents' attention. I always felt he was Mom's favorite. Even then, I was my Dad's favorite. When parents have favorites, and the kids know, it can be hurtful to the little ones. Knowing that God loved me got me through the tough times.

Wayne was the only boy in our family with dark hair, like my dad. He would be drafted into the Army during the Vietnam War when he got older. Using the GI Bill, he went to college in Tennessee, settled down, and married the "love of his life." He still resides in Tennessee.

I was my parent's second child. Can you imagine my mom's surprise? Perhaps that's why she sent us to school at an early age—just because she could. Mom was the second youngest, so she didn't have to care for her younger sister.

Fortunately, Wayne and I were good playmates. Aunt Marge and my cousin, Jimmy, lived next door. Jimmy was a week older than me. I remember walking to the creek and wading in the water with him along with my brother. With my brother being just a little bit older and having a lot of cousins who were older boys, I tried to do whatever they did. I remember once being on a wall, and they jumped. So, I jumped. I still have the stitch marks on my chin and marks on my knees and both ankles from hitting the unpaved road. Later during my preteen years, we played in the streets with the other neighbor kids. We played Red Light, Green Light, and Hide and Seek. We would also play kickball, hopscotch, and hula hoops.

Aunt Marge had a large family: three boys and then her girl. Later, she moved to a one-story house about five minutes away, and she would babysit for my sister Carole's baby girl.

The third child was a sister three and a half years younger than me. I remember her as always being a polite and obedient child. When I was much older and began my period (what we called "my friend"), Dad would complain about me being cranky. "Why can't you be like Janet? She's so polite and has a good demeanor." (Janet and I both had light hair like Mom. If people hadn't seen us for a while, they might mistake us for each other as we really did look like sisters).

When Janet finished high school, she stayed in Pittsburgh. Mom and Dad, who didn't have the money to put her through college, gave her a choice to become a secretary or nurse. Because none of us girls liked blood, she chose to be a secretary.

She landed a good job working for Westinghouse and later went to college at night to earn her degree and advance in her field. She had the same position as an engineer: supplying her customers with nuclear power plant parts!

Carole was the last child. She was nine years

younger than me and had coal-black hair, like Dad. I believe she was a surprise baby. It wasn't my mom's midlife crisis, but I don't think my mom was ready to raise such a large family. Mom didn't come home when Carole was born. She went from the regular hospital to the state hospital. Big Al and his wife, Viola, who lived across the street, raised Carole for her first six months.

Most of the time growing up, we girls shared a bedroom. Can you imagine three girls (two of whom were teens) sharing one small closet and one dresser? We three also slept in one double bed. I was sixteen years old before I got my bedroom for one year before graduating high school. I had it painted a purple hue.

I often stayed at Aunt Rosalie's (my dad's sister's) house for a week during the summer. I was in my preteens. Her small cottage-like house had three bedrooms. One was a makeshift bedroom in the basement. (That was Grandpa's room after Grandma died). She had two children of her own. Her daughter Audrey was at least five years older than me, but she played with me as if I were her doll. I remember her putting curlers in my hair. Uncle Roy used to call me his "curly, whirlybird." (I was delighted that someone curled my hair and loved the attention).

Growing up, we only had a few communications with Grandma and Grandpa. Shortly after Grandma died, Grandpa moved in with my Aunt Rosalie. Even though he stayed with her the most, he tried to spend a week in rotation with each of his other children. Later, when my mother became ill, he would stay with us for longer than a week.

I grew up over fifty years ago, so parents raised children differently. For example, my brother and I shared some of the same toys and friends. I remember learning to ride his "boy bike." It was painful riding at times because I had shorter legs. It was more than awkward when I would fall on the thick, metal middle bar. It hurt! And because our home was one of the first built on our block, the street was not paved. I still have scars on my ankles and knees from falling.

My brother was more friendly than me and had some charm with the teachers, but I was the more academic one. When I started school, it was easy for the teachers to see how different I was. Later, during our teen years, listening to music with him and his friends was fun. I even had a crush on at least one. He liked a friend of mine as well.

Once, when we were on the way home from a family reunion in the country, my brother and I hid a cute and cuddly puppy in the backseat of our car. One of our relatives was giving away six-week-old puppies, and we were sure that Dad would let us keep him once he found out and warmed up to the idea. To our surprise, Dad didn't let us keep him! Instead, our Aunt Stella gladly took him. She later told us that he was the best dog she ever had!

Growing up, our favorite family pastime was going to the drive-in movie theater. Mom would pop a big pot of popcorn, bring a couple of liters of soda, and maybe some other snack. We children always looked forward to playing on the playground before the cartoons started. Our favorite spot to sit was on the inside ledge of the station wagon, looking at the screen over the top of the car, our feet dangling on the inside. I can still picture it. It was one of the highlights of our summers, and we often went there instead of away on vacations.

The drive-in permitted persons to view the movies from their car, which were projected on a giant screen made of wood and painted white. It must have been thirty feet tall by sixty feet wide! The gravel-paved lot appeared to cover several acres. At some drive-ins, a playground was found at the front bottom of the screen to accommodate the energetic children before the start of the movie or at intermission. Some drive-ins were charged by the carload and others by the number of persons in the car.

The wide outside theatre comprised at least thirty gravel-covered acres and had row after row of twin speakers about twenty feet apart and drive-through lanes every hundred feet or so. The speakers were on the slightly elevated part of the lanes facing the screen, so the car was tilted at fifteen to twenty degrees toward the screen.

Each car pulled up on the left or right side of the four-foot-high posts that held the two wired speakers. Each had plastic handles or clips to hang inside the vehicle's windows. Volume control was standard. Some had a call button to talk to office staff.

Some drive-ins had two or three movies, but some had only one if it was a highly popular film. The privacy of viewing films from inside your vehicle also permitted romance, which was likely the selling point of the drive-in. The price was also more affordable to larger families!

Several times, I spent a week for a mini-vacation with Aunt Stella, my mom's sister, who lived just seven miles away. My cousins had a community pool nearby, which meant swimming. Aunt Stella was the matriarch of Mom's side of the family and taught me structure by having me do chores. Evidently, she perceived that I needed some semblance of everyday family life because she was the one who helped Mom keep the house during her illnesses. Mom's poor health made it hard for her to keep any schedule at home, so Aunt Stella knew how disorganized it could get.

Now, I did have clean clothes and hot meals at night. However, I never noticed how different our family was from Aunt Stella's or other "normal" families. Dad worked so much when we were young but only managed to provide for necessities. Mom's hospital bills ate up any savings we might have used for vacations, extra housecleaning for Mom, or even an in-ground swimming pool. As it was, any of these things that we wanted involved working hard for them.

Dad built our stone house and double garage. Later, he built an in-ground pool with a decorative stone wall surrounding it. That made us very popular with relatives during swim season! And when they came, they didn't bring anything to share with us, from towels to food. Big Al across the street maintained our pool, and his daughter, Diana, enjoyed the pool, too.

Of the few childhood memories I have of my mom, one fond memory was a special "Ladies" Night at the Pittsburgh Pirates Baseball Game" that we had with two neighbor ladies. It was exciting to see Bill Mazursky and Roberto Clemente hit home runs, and they always did! Afterward, we would each eat a hot Reuben sandwich at a local restaurant. I'm sure my other younger sisters had time with Mom, especially after I left for college, but I can't seem to remember.

2

Light Reading on a Dark Subject

I believe I got a love for God from my Grandma (my dad's mom). She was a woman of prayer who would pray fervently for her children and grandchildren. When she had time for that, I don't know because she had thirteen children (two died in childbirth). My dad loved music, could play the harmonica and violin, and loved to perform. He once performed in high school doing a jig while playing the violin. He later learned the banjo and mandolin. He also wrote several songs with his sister-in-law, Elaine. I get my performance genes from him, I guess.

Grandma and Grandpa lived on a farm and were very religious and strict (aside from the dancing). I'm sure they had to be to keep to some schedule with all of their children. The girls were born first, and then the boys.

I was named after both of my grandmothers. One grandmother was a Carrie, and the other was Catherine. Blended, they got Karen, which means *pure one.* The irony of that name's meaning in so many ways is not wasted on me.

Busha was Polish for "grandma," and that's what we called my mom's stepmother. I never met Mom's real mom and dad, as they died before I was born. I did know Mom's two older sisters, two older brothers, and one younger sister. The youngest was the only one out of her siblings to get a divorce. Her husband left her and married somebody else. She ended up single and had to work as a nurse's aide and cleaning lady. That's probably why my mom stuck with my dad for fifty-four years of marriage: she didn't want to end up like her sister. She never complained!

As a child, knowing that God loved me and I loved him was a huge comfort during times when I felt abandoned by Dad, being overworked or ignored by Mom constantly being sick. One memory comes to mind.

Once, my brother and I were cooking in the kitchen. I don't remember what we were making, but he had a knife, and I had a larger knife. For some reason, we were playing around, and I accidentally nicked his finger, which started bleeding. We rushed into the bathroom to clean it up and get a Band Aid. I hated looking at blood, but I knew where the Band Aids were and could help find them quickly.

But then something happened that I didn't understand for a long time. While we were in the bathroom with the door closed, getting my brother bandaged up, Mom started yelling something nasty at us through the door. She was having an episode that scared us so badly that we locked the door. That didn't help and provoked her even more, so she started shouting, "What are you doing in there?"

Somebody must have dialed the emergency number to call the ambulance at this point because they showed up pretty fast. I remember them coming in with a stretcher and strapping Mom down, putting belts on her legs and arms so that she couldn't move. And all the while, Mom was still yelling. Our living room was only large enough for the stretcher and a few helpers. We were too afraid to unlock the door at first. The last my brother and I saw of her for a while was Mom on the stretcher. I don't remember how long she was gone after that incident, but I might have been in sixth grade. She left for a time when I was in the sixth and seventh grades. However, she wasn't gone as long as she was when one of my sisters was born. I was in the fourth grade then.

I did hear that they shocked Mom with electrodes. She lost some of her memory, but the procedure worked to calm her, along with the pills that made her sleep. After coming home, she wasn't awake most of the time. When I got dressed for school, no one brushed my hair. I also had no bows to go in my hair. Our house was so unorganized that I'm not even sure we had a place to put a hairbrush.

I had to learn to dress myself at a young age and lacked awareness of what was appropriate, like dressing for the weather. Sometimes, I wore short sleeves when I should have worn long sleeves, and the kids would make fun of me. But at least there weren't any major happenings with my mom during high school. I think my mom might have gone to the hospital for a few days to adjust her meds. I remember crying because I hadn't finished my homework.

One of my favorite childhood memories was the leftover DeCarlo pizza from Mom's Pinochle Club. With four kids in the house, someone else would eat it if you didn't. Sometimes, Mom would heat the leftover pizza in a skillet, which made it crispy at the bottom. If there were any leftover pizza, my brother and I could be seen eating it on the way to school. Talking about food, we used to eat ten-cent burgers on Tuesdays at the BullPen. It didn't stay open long, perhaps a year or two. The Health Department shut it down as they didn't like their menu. Rumor had it that they had discovered it was horse meat or kangaroo meat!

Mom loved to garden, but she didn't like weeding. She would offer each of us kids a quarter to weed, which was a lot of money then. Five cents would buy a giant Hershey bar! Mom even paid us to fold those socks and find their missing matches. She turned everything into a game and rewarded us for helping her. Sometimes, when there were lots of weeds, she would engage neighbor kids to help us and pay them too. (That was probably her tip money, as she started as a waitress just a few hours at some point).

When Dad relaxed a little more on weekends, he planted beautiful roses for Mom on the side of the house. Later in life, he grew tomatoes, which were always perfect. He was proud to give many away.

I told you that Rosalie's dad, Grandpa, lived with her after her mom died. She also invited the new in-laws (who would have been my ex) to stay with her the weekend of my wedding. I remember writing a thank you note, saying, "I never realized how small your house was because you had such a big heart." She loved that, and it was so true.

A note on our house growing up. Next to us appeared an empty lot, designated as a future roadway, but it was never developed. So we planted grass and maintained it. As kids, we used it as an extra part of our yard for baseball, croquet, or any needed activity. We called it "the alleyway," but it was all grassy and lovely.

But there came a time when Dad and Mom were so busy with their own issues that they weren't paying attention to me as carefully as they might have otherwise. During this time, I knew I wasn't a bad person, per se. However, bad things happened to me.

A close family member abused me for several years. I cried. I even prayed. But it didn't stop (Somehow, my brother knew but never told me until he was an adult). I have often tried to reconstruct the circumstances as to why the abuse started in the first place. Had I done something wrong? Did I deserve to be treated that way?

Because of the abuse and decades of trauma that followed, I don't recall the specifics of the abuse. But I also can't remember many fun-filled childhood memories. There are literally large sections of my childhood that have been wiped from my memory. When I hear my older brother describe events that happened or even something as simple as washing dishes with Mom, I'm embarrassed to say that I don't recall any of this. Perhaps the evil done to me overshadowed the good.

I later learned that this memory loss is a symptom of post-traumatic stress disorder (PTSD). I had been troubled for many years, wondering why my family life differed from other wholesome families. Instead of fun-filled memories at birthday parties, Christmases, and Thanksgiving dinners around the table, anger, yelling, and name-calling dominate my memory bank as a regular part of family interactions. I got the belt and not the fist, as my brother did. It surprised me that whenever Dad would get into his enraged discipline sessions, Mom would freeze because she didn't know what to do. It also amazes me that she stayed with Dad through these nasty times. I remember being surprised when Mom yelled, "Stop!" when Dad hit too long. It stopped Dad long enough for us children to run in the opposite direction.

Later on, as an adult, somebody enlightened me on why Dad might have gone into frequent uncontrollable rages against us children. I learned that my father abused alcohol early in my parents' marriage. Before that, however, his father also disciplined him in the same way. This is called "conditioning." If not examined, conditioned behaviors can continue without understanding when or why. Little did I know as a child that my dad's behavior, along with my mom's dismissiveness, was not normal family life or the one I deserved.

Growing up, the neighbors in our neighborhood were primarily Catholic. Remember how, as a child, I knew that God loved me? When I learned that things weren't normal in our house or even bearable, I prayed that my family would attend the Catholic church together. Maybe that was what my family needed. After all, Mom raised us Catholic even though Dad didn't attend any church. After years of praying that God would have my family attend the Catholic church, I finally got my answer—but not the one I expected.

When Dad was young, he attended a small Pentecostal church. It wasn't strict like many churches in that denomination are. Church members could play cards and games, and the women wore slacks.

There was no liquor in our house. Well, Dad did drink when we were younger, but when Dad got saved, liquor was forbidden in our home. Mom occasionally sneaked a small drink with her lady friends or sisters at their house. I remember tasting alcohol at Uncle Chester's Christmas party. We cousins hid in the dark while the adults gathered in another room. It made me sleepy.

I never smoked cigarettes, though Dad and Mom did in their early years. I did try to make a cigarette as a young teenager by rolling a newspaper like a cigar and lighting the end of it. That didn't end well when the fire came into my mouth! Yeah. It scared me.

At some point, Dad forbade us to attend the Catholic church. Why? I don't know the specifics, but he didn't believe in Catholicism. So, my brother and I would walk a mile and a half to St. Norbert's Catholic Church while Dad worked a second job to pay the bills. I'm unsure if Mom took my younger sisters to church. Later, my brother and I would only go on special Catholic holidays if Dad was home.

Finally, desperate to attend church, I tried a different tactic.

"Dad, take us to your church." That did the trick. He dropped us off at his church to work an extra job.

After six months of attending the Protestant Church, I realized that I wasn't "saved" and forgiven of my sins. That meant that I wasn't going to heaven either. (There was too much church jargon for me to understand. From that day on, I was determined to share my faith in simple words so the average unchurched person could understand).

One Sunday evening before church camp, Pastor Raynor delivered a message of such power. I rushed to the altar and surrendered my life to God by confessing my sins and asking Jesus to come into my heart. My dad and middle sister also prayed a similar prayer. From that night forward, life was new for us.

3

Behold, All Things Have Become New

Mom and my younger sister joined us soon after. At first, Mom's sisters shunned her leaving Catholicism, but later, they realized it was best for her marriage and family. Dad found a gentler demeanor, stopped drinking, and came home for supper at night.

A month later, my parents coerced my brother Wayne to attend church to get his driver's license. During a special week of revival with a guest preacher, he also confessed his sin and new faith with a noticeable lifestyle change. Together, Wayne at sixteen and I at fifteen, ignited the youth group with our enthusiasm for the Lord. He was elected president, and I was his vice-president. We also joined Youth for Christ and memorized scriptures. Competing on a Bible Quiz team, we both won second place.

We were taught how to share our faith with others, and we did that, whether door-to-door or just in our everyday lives. Together, we started a Bible Study group in our high school.

And then, imagine: the pastor asked my father to be a Deacon at church and a board member for Youth for Christ! And I was allowed to go to Ocean City, New Jersey, with Youth for Christ. (In our family of four children, three being teens, we didn't have any extra funds for vacations). They offered me a "job working in their office, stuffing envelopes and other menial tasks" for the price of my trip! That includes breakfast and dinner, lodging, and the bus trip there and back. An unexpected blessing, indeed. Someone should have mentioned that the trip did not include lunch or extra spending money. I don't remember if I fasted or someone paid for my lunch. (Probably a little of both). Even on the long bus trip (four or five hours), I remember sharing my faith and several teens accepting Jesus as their Lord and Savior with a commitment of faith. There was no fear of sharing my faith—just zeal and holy boldness to share the good news. (Later, an adult, seeing my enthusiasm, said, "May you never lose your zeal for the LORD!" Thank you for the seed you planted in my heart and mind many years ago).

During that beach week, there was a college night highlighting Christian Colleges in the U.S. I chose several schools in Pennsylvania and later visited two of them, Philadelphia School of the Bible and Messiah College. I chose the latter because of its pastoral setting in Central Pennsylvania and being closer to Pittsburgh. I enrolled at age seventeen with an Elementary Education Major.

Coming home from college that first summer, I did something wrong. I can't even remember what, but Dad took off his leather belt and was preparing to give me a whack. I guess that hadn't stopped—it just lessened quite a bit. I screamed through the open bedroom window, and he left immediately without using his belt. That was the last time he dared to take the belt to me (the following summer, I chose to work at a summer camp away from home).

It's no wonder I married at twenty, but I loved my man. We were young with "much baggage" and poor communication skills. Later, with much counseling (thirteen years or so), I realized the abuse I had suffered left me with PTSD. As a result, I needed even more counseling as a prerequisite to getting married.

Might I interject that I had the "best Mom" that she knew how to be? She loved us children dearly, but because her parents died young, she was raised strictly by her brothers and two older sisters. When my dad was unloving and unfaithful in their early years of marriage, Mom had several mental breakdowns. She was held for six months in a state hospital immediately after my youngest sister was born (not covered by medical insurance at that time). The neighbors, Al and Viola, cared for her as their own. (They had only one other daughter, about five at the time). I was nine and in the fourth grade. Dad declared bankruptcy as he was a contractor building houses at the time. Although these hospital stays continued during my sixth, seventh, and ninth grades, they were not lengthy.

Grandpa (Dad's dad) visited for the first month, making meals and giving us chores. Eventually, Grandpa and Dad couldn't continue to live together. We were alone except for Mom's sister, Aunt Stella, who would collect laundry to wash and iron and help us get back on schedule. Aunt Stella had her own family of three children and a husband to care for. Everyone tried to "put our house back in order." It worked for a season, but Mom couldn't function on eight hours of sleep. She was on meds that made her sleepy, and no one could put our home back into shape for any length of time. (Dad had started working a second and third job, and Mom worked as a short-order cook when she could.)

Looking at my school pictures, you may notice no bow or ribbon in my hair. None of us girls had hair accessories. Like I've said already, we didn't even have a special place for a hairbrush, if we had one at all. I don't blame my mom. She did her best, but she needed her sleep and those meds to function.

I wish we had family portraits with matching outfits. (I guess that would have looked out of place with our messy hairdos). We didn't have any family portraits in our early years. Later, as adults, we managed to get together for a nice picture.

In my teen years, I felt confident in my appearance. Mom helped me get babysitting jobs and sold Avon and Fuller Brush with her as my sponsor. With extra funds I could buy my clothes. I loved to dance and usually had a boyfriend. I wasn't into sports or cheerleading, which required taking the late activity bus home. It was already dark and a scary walk home from our last bus stop by then. I joined the Pep Club and was elected president and later Pep Queen in my senior year. Jack, whom I had just led to the Lord, accompanied me. (He lived across the street from where I was babysitting). Many years later, he's still serving the Lord as Assistant Pastor of his church.

During those early teen years, I learned to pray with an elderly lady from church, Sister Kerns. I would call her after the children, who I was babysitting, were asleep. We would share a little and then start praying and "reaching heaven." Wow, they were powerful prayers. I could feel God's presence! The Lord was beginning to heal my wounded heart!

Shortly after I left for college, my brother was drafted into the Army and sent to Vietnam. Later, he would use the GI Bill to go to Lee College and earn his bachelor's degree in Ministry and later a Counseling Degree. (Perhaps he changed to understand Mom's mental illness better). Jack drove three-and-a-half hours to pick me up at college to see my brother before he left the country. That's seven hours for each trip in the winter over the snowy mountains.

Wow, what a friend! He was my brother's best friend.

***

CELL PHONE ACCIDENTS *That Have Happened to Me*

1. *Immersed in clean water,* on the wet sink, or dropped in a bucket of water.

2. *Immersed in sweat water,* too close to a sweat gland while riding my bike.

3. *Immersed in ocean water.* It slid down my pocketless pants and fell into the water as I walked. A wave took it, but a guy caught it. I ran toward him and shouted, "That's my phone!" I set it in the sun to dry and never lost a message or contact!

4. *Immersed in dirty water* (as in toilet water). It just slipped out of my back pocket too quickly.

5. *By running over it with my car.* Chad set it on the roof of the vehicle. I drove away and later noticed pieces of it strewn on the road. "Is this your phone?" B asked. "No, mine had numbers on it," which we found on the side of the next road.

6. *Or leave it SOMEWHERE, where I ate a quick meal, at the farmer's market, in a store, almost anywhere.*

7. *I did drop it on my apartment floor as I left to fly to Tennessee to see my brother.* I had to get back to work the following day. A storm caused a lot of delays. I changed my flight to Baltimore rather than Chicago. I hitched a ride with an ex-military guy who drove me home, afraid that I might lose my job if I missed a day of work (I used his phone to alert my friend, Judee, who had my house key). Stupid, I know. She prayed & I stayed awake till we got there. I promised never to take a ride with a stranger again. Diana, a friend at work, made me promise to call her in an emergency like that!

Trust in the Lord with all your heart
and lean not on your own understanding;
in all your ways acknowledge him, and he
will make your paths straight.

—Proverbs 3:5-6

The Lord is my strength and my shield;
my heart trusts in him, and he helps me.
My heart leaps for joy, and with my song
I praise him.

Psalm 28:7 (NIV)

Part II

Mrs. Karen

Early Adulthood

4

Looking for Love Too Soon

I felt fortunate to go to a small Christian college, and I did get a small scholarship. Meanwhile, Dad had made a career change from building houses to selling insurance. He struggled to pay the bills with one job, so he worked a bricklaying job on the weekends. While my brother was in Vietnam, Dad could use my brother's newer, more dependable car. Since Mom's health was good during this time, she was able to work a part-time job. I was not aware of their great sacrifice at that time. I had a small income from the work-study program to meet my frugal needs. I had no access to a car, so there was little temptation to shop, as no public transportation was available. I was the first in my family to attend college. Each sibling did attend, and three of us earned degrees.

My first trip to college after my acceptance was

memorable. Our car broke down shortly after leaving the Pennsylvania Turnpike, just five miles before our destiny. Our car was towed to a small town garage in Mechanicsburg. The kind owner of Zimmerman's Auto Body Shop lent us a car for the weekend until they could repair ours. We drove into the small town at a dingy little restaurant to have lunch. The food was awful, and the water was the worst I had ever tasted. I remember declaring, "I'd never want to live here." Fast forward three years later: I married and settled outside that very town and kept the address of Mechanicsburg for over thirty-five years!

It's almost laughable that I would write a book, as my first composition in College English received an F. F for Failure, not Fabulous! I had trouble with verb tense and spelling.

Young people, this was before spell-check and Google. No one had computers then. I say all that to make the point that I never considered myself a writer. I'd rather give a speech or talk in front of any group. Ironically, I met Chad in speech class. But I finally earned my A in composition!

During my first semester, I had one or two dates. To keep busy on weekends, I often participated in campus activities. Most of the students lived close and could go home on weekends. About twenty students were left, so it was lonely on the weekends. Even my roommate Ann went home every week. However, no one ever invited me. By Thanksgiving break, I was ready to go home. My plane flight was scheduled for early evening, and most students had left earlier in the day. A few were attending the Wednesday night church meeting. A young couple entered the dorm, and I asked, "How do you get to the airport?"

“Well, do you have a car?”

"No. I think my driver forgot about me!" I cried as tears rolled down my cheeks. "We can take you," they answered, and off we went. I think I hugged him. He was running for student council, and he got my vote! Yes, he won!

We had a wonderful weekend, but Dad delayed our trip due to inclement weather. Some of my dorm friends thought I dropped out. I should have called someone, but I was only a day late.

***

Lessons I Learned *From My Mom*

1. *I'm trying my best.* Accept me as I am.
2. *Kind words to all.* I never heard Mom say a bad thing about her family or friends.
3. *Choose your friends wisely.* She warned us to avoid those with a bad reputation.

4. *Be thankful for what you have*—for example, a roof over your head, a warm home, food, etc.

5. *Make do with what you have.* Whether food, clothes, or anything that you can afford.

6. *Hard work never hurt anyone.*

7. *Love your husband by respecting him.* She respected Dad. His word was gold as he earned the money. She would always refer to him as "My Bob," as if "Hollywood" was his last name. That could be a reference to how he signed his cards to Mom: "Love, Robert Redford."

8. *Always do your best!* She encouraged us to do well in school even though she had yet to finish high school (few people did back then). She wanted us to get better jobs.

9. Mom loved God and her family. She encouraged us to go to church and boy, did she pray!

10. Mom knew how to have fun. She was the life of the party in her younger, healthier years. Some would say I learned that well!

11. *Look your best when you go somewhere!* For Mom, that meant clean, fresh clothes, makeup, and lipstick! Oh, and, *Buy at least one new top or dress each year.*

***

Incentives

For Children and Teens

1. Use rewards!
2. Take pride in a job well done.
3. Save for a "rainy day."
4. Each one has unique talents given to us by God.
5. Always praise for good job, deed, or behavior.
6. A hug or other appropriate show of affection.
7. A favorite meal or dessert.
8. Spending time together.
9. Surprises! Knowing their interests.

***

Returning to the library where I worked, I saw Chad, an upperclassman in my speech class. He smiled and talked a few minutes before asking me to attend the following special event on campus. I was shocked at first as I answered, "With whom?" Then I added that I didn't have a formal dress. (That wasn't the "yes" he was expecting, but it wasn't a "no" either). When I returned to the dorm, I asked several people if they knew him. My dorm leader did and attested that he was a dependable gentleman. (He's the one who typed the morning newsletter each day). Then I inquired if anyone had an extra dress. I found one my size! I responded that I would like to go with him. My original answer was part of the first prank gift Chad would give me before Christmas break (a sock puppet and plastic ring with a note from Charlie). We survived that first impression with an enjoyable dinner and several college activities together.

With a long four-week Christmas break between semesters, I hadn't heard from Chad until a dozen red roses were delivered. Imagine my shock! Shortly after our first date, he told a neighbor that I was the one he would marry. Impressed, I still wasn't convinced at that point.

Chad was part of the basketball team, yet we continued to enjoy each other's company around his schedule. However, the following year, he enrolled in business classes at Temple University, our satellite campus. I'm unsure of the exact details, but we were "separated as a couple" for a period. We resolved the misunderstanding, and by summer, we were both camp counselors away from home. But then he left and took a job making more money in his hometown.

That next school year, I enrolled in our Temple University campus to be close and experience city life in Philadelphia with him. Chad became a full-time Temple student with his apartment around the corner of our complex.

Interestingly, we took turns cooking, a paid position. My first meal included baking six pumpkin pies. With no baking experience, my pie crust was hard rather than soft and crumbly. I don't recall anyone complaining, as we all took turns cooking!

Temple was in a dangerous section of Philadelphia. You could have your tires stolen if you parked too long in a spot. I had $40 stolen by young boys in the neighborhood who found an open door in our complex one day. There was a knife incident while we traveled a block to the library and later a gang killing in the same block where we lived. We didn't watch the news, so we found out later when we were safe in our "secluded area."

After the first semester in Philly, Chad joined me at Christmas in Pittsburgh at my parents' home and gave me an engagement ring (we picked it out earlier). He was just a few years older than me but only one year ahead of me in college.

He landed a good job immediately after college and housing so we could get married the summer before my senior year. At twenty, I had never lived independently and was unprepared for married life, but it was an escape from home. Though I loved him, I was immature in many ways. Both of us had baggage from our families and very poor communication skills. We managed to work through those early years with some guidance. And I did finish my degree as planned the following school year. My parents came to my graduation but were puzzled when they didn't hear my name called. They had yet to anticipate my married name.

For decades, I've been writing daily in a journal. So, writing has become a process even as my life has evolved. Ironically, the LORD would want me to write a book. He put it in my heart to attend writing conferences and clubs. However, I could only journal because I was in the middle of a crisis. There was no way I could concentrate on writing a book. Now that I'm retired and not exactly a spring chicken, I have found the time. Take one step at a time, and the path will be more apparent with God's guidance.

May the favor of the Lord our God rest on us;
establish the work of our hands for us—
yes, establish the work of our hands.

PSALM 90:17 (NIV)

PART III

Mommy Karen

MOTHERHOOD

5

Tangled Up in the Knot I Tied

Since my schedule was more sporadic, my husband found an alternative means of transportation, sharing a ride to work. I drove our only car to college for class. We were able to purchase a fully-furnished used mobile home just a mile from the college. It was in an adult-only section (no children living in that area). We lived simply within our budget. Living in the mobile home seemed cozy for the first few years. There was little maintenance inside or out until one brutal winter. The winds howled through the windows and shook our very being. That night, the pipes froze under the mobile home. Little did we know we were supposed to wrap the pipes to prevent freezing! It was scary, and we decided we didn't want to make this home permanent.

Before having children, we made friends with another couple near us, Joyce and Rick, enjoying time together at a local park. We had weekly visits from Chad's family or visited Gettysburg and his grandparents' home when parents, cousins, aunts, and uncles came. That wasn't easy the first year of our marriage as I was still a college student, but that didn't seem to matter to them. (Perhaps Chad and I should have had that conversation). As a result, my grades suffered a tad. It was challenging to balance our lives together.

Meanwhile, my parents and family lived three-and-a-half hours away. They didn't visit often, maybe once a year. We would visit on long holiday weekends. The church family became our family to confide in and guide us. We would gravitate toward a few couples who were older and wiser than us. There were always activities there.

Chad kept his doctor and dentist in Gettysburg for over ten years. That way, he could stay and visit his mother longer. His two brothers married and moved further away. The older one moved just outside Washington, D. C., where they worked. In contrast, the younger brother moved to a nearby town about thirty minutes away. (It was still close enough for him to have his mom babysit while they worked). It was rare for us to ask his parents to babysit. (Chad's dad died on Adam's third birthday, so Chad would feel the need to drive his mom to our home and back, a 120-mile round trip. Yet she had no problem driving to the younger son's place about the same distance. They had a bond that the other sons didn't have.

After I graduated, I would become more active in the church, teaching Sunday School class. I taught junior high, and Chad taught the senior high students. Later, he was elected to the Board with other responsibilities, and I helped in various women's ministries. We hosted a couple of missionary women in our new home for a week. After two years working as a Department Manager of a large department store, Chad secured a job working for the Federal Government at the Mechanicsburg Navy Depot. We were far from any body of water, but they provided a logistic support system. It was closer to our home, with weekends and holidays off. A better job and pay!

A year later, when I worked full-time teaching elementary students, we were able to save money for a new home. This time we decided to move to the country to a huge lot. We could take our used furniture from the mobile home to our new house. We only stayed there for two years because of several issues with the property. It's too bad we couldn't take our new neighbors, Carolyn and Bob, with us. Carolyn taught me a lot about home cooking and many other homemaking skills. We stayed in touch for several years.

I'll never forget our long double-car driveway covered with snow. One school day, we shoveled side by side for an hour just in time to get in our cars to go to work. Another time, our road was closed for three days due to a heavy snowstorm. That had to be the worst snowstorm with the most enormous driveway ever! I promised to keep working until we could move into a better home closer to town. Then, we would start a family.

Meanwhile, I went back to graduate school to continue my master's degree as a Reading Specialist, and Chad decided to get a master's degree also, this time in counseling. However, he has yet to pursue a career in that field. I was required to earn twenty-four graduate credits, but a master's degree was only two more classes. (His degree was not a necessity as he didn't get any extra salary, nor did he use his knowledge. Perhaps his insecurity showed through later when a professor encouraged me to get my doctorate. Chad balked and said, "You choose me or the degree.")

I started teaching first grade, then three years of third grade, and I taught second grade for the last two years. The district moved teachers from grade to grade. When I chose to teach the third grade again, I had to move to another school within the district. They closed that school the following year, so I returned to my first school after they expanded it. I say that to explain how I was overlooked by so many around me to have a baby shower after waiting seven years. Only some teachers knew me, as the school had doubled in size, and half of them were newly hired. Instead, they took a collection of a dollar or so and bought a small umbrella stroller. I appreciated it, though having a baby shower to celebrate would have been nice. (I received an extra gift from one of my co-workers and a few individuals close to me). Even my students gave me small gifts. Billy gave me a fifty-cent coin, and that meant a big sacrifice!

My belly was so huge that my doctor thought I was going to deliver a month earlier than originally planned. That meant I couldn't travel to Pittsburgh, close to my family. A teen from church wanted to have a shower for me, but that didn't happen. My mother-in-law said, "Well, I didn't have one for Sharon (the oldest daughter-in-law), so I can't show favoritism."

Karen and Jeff were great friends. We met in our Lamaze class while I was pregnant. We happened to be at the same hospital when our boys were born in March. She came in two days after me. Since we both had C-sections, we were there for a week. We were nursing our boys, so we put them "on hold" while we played backgammon a few times. We also stayed in touch with another couple, Linda and Steve, whom we had met in Lamaze Class. We all had boys, and we'd get together for several years.

While at home, I worked various part-time jobs. Several friends asked me to babysit their children before or after school, and my sons enjoyed the companionship. I became active in the community as well as the church. Another woman asked me to help start a food bank in our local church. I remember getting day-old bread from a local bakery to distribute to needy families. Before taking the load to the church, I would drop off several loaves of bread and rolls to my neighbor with twelve children!

Later, I started a prayer chapter with Concerned Women for America (CWA) as we represented the family's concerns in government. At some point, I was the Representative/leader for central Pennsylvania and later the state leader when the Pittsburgh leader moved. Holding rallies at the state capital, Harrisburg (as we lived only fifteen minutes away) was exciting. I would bribe my young sons to accompany me and then take them to the Museum of Scientific Discovery, where we had a family membership. (I had attended training sessions in Washington, D.C. with Beverly La Haye and several conservative politicians like Newt Gingrich, Bob Dole, and more). Local news interviewed me to represent the Pro-life position on local television.

The first time I was on television, the news was unplanned. Sarah accompanied me to a local community meeting that was opposing an X-rated porn store from coming to their local area. She prayed that the LORD would be with me and grant me favor to speak. And He did. I was able to speak when handed several microphones.

Little did I know that I would be on several local news stations that evening announcing our Rally for Decency at the capital and the start of the WRAP (White Ribbons Against Pornography) campaign.

At the time, I was asked to be the chairperson for my county. I wasn't even sure how large our county was, but I found out. I had plenty of help, especially from the Catholic churches, other churches, and our community. It was a successful venture for several years.

At some point, I was so busy with community activities that I had to spend more time with my young family. A young military couple asked me to evaluate her two son's homeschooling portfolios. That led me to attend the Pennsylvania Homeschool Conference to research and become an evaluator. My sons eventually asked me to homeschool them, so I also researched that. Before starting to teach them, I enlisted a tutor for Bryte in basic reading skills that summer. That was the beginning of an adventure.

6

Career Woman, Mom, Or Both?

When my boys were young, we visited the library for story hour and church for Sunday school classes. I loved how my boys shared all of their toys because they were close in age to play together. We bought a wooden toy train set that we would add to it every year. It was pretty expensive, so we bought a new addition or two each Christmas. They learned to improvise very early.

There was a little merry-go-round outside the old Kmart, and I would put my boys on the horses, and they would "ride." But it didn't move on its own. I was the one doing the moving! I didn't put any money in, but they didn't know. They were as "happy as larks" to sit on those horses until one year, when they saw someone put a quarter in, all the horses started moving. I was caught!

The boys enjoyed each other, and they did everything together. I remember they made tents out of blankets by draping them over a couple of chairs. Chase learned to skate in the basement, which still needed to be finished. Chase learned to balance at a young age by riding a scooter. One day, he got a bicycle with training wheels, and the next day, he told us that we could take them off. And he could ride it because he had such good balance after riding the scooter.

When I would get the boys treats, I would buy one candy bar or small bag of candy, and they would share. We would go to the community swimming pool, and they would have popsicles we would buy for a nickel each. (Imagine last vacation, I paid $5 or $7 for half of one).

We bought the boys toys like Lincoln Logs and Legos. When they lost interest in their toys, they would start building in the backyard with things like the big logs used for landscaping today. They once made a cabin two levels high and put in some fold-up chairs. We removed a small red maple tree that was too close to the house. And before we could plant a new one, the boys turned it into a miniature hole-in-one golf course. One of the neighbors said, "I can't believe you let your kids do that." I said, "Well, why not? There was a hole there already." So, I was lenient on them when it came to these kinds of things. I loved the idea that these things were relatively inexpensive and very innovative.

Shortly after the movie *Home Alone,* where the young boy escapes using a makeshift swing, our boys had a great idea. They used the handlebars from a scooter that may have been broken. I don't know if I still believe that story these many years later. They connected a rope from one tree to another, which worked for a little bit. I wasn't too happy because it was over my shade garden, and I had plans to show that garden one year. Fast forward twenty-five years, and Adam made a real swing, including a safety harness and pulley in his backyard for his girls. Amazing and fun!

Every year, I asked my colleague, a friend who was part of the sunflower garden tour, whether or not he thought it was time to show my garden. My shade garden was over one hundred feet long and filled with a variety of hostas, daylilies, and other shade plants. I did a lot of planting after the oldest went to college. Finally, Chad helped dig the perimeter while I planted. We also put in a walkway alongside the house to the back patio.

My mom would visit us for one week during the summer when the boys were small. In her early years, she was in excellent health and would even play baseball with the boys and run around the bases that we put in the cul de sac. Both Grandmothers tried to jump on their trampoline, which took up a fourth of our backyard. The boys would put a sprinkler underneath the trampoline to keep themselves cool and became very popular with the neighborhood kids.

Like I said, the boys enjoyed each other. The younger two, Bryte and Chase, shared a room. Bryte kept everything neat and organized, and Chase, who was more adventuresome, was not so organized. Because Bryte was very particular about everything, it was advantageous at some point for us to add on to the house so that each could have his own room.

When Chad traveled for work, the boys and I would have a fun time—some fun activities. We had the Museum of Discovery annual pass for several years. When I homeschooled, I took them to all kinds of parks, museums, and landmarks. There were art classes and free concerts at Dickinson College. We invited others to join our organized time together. We even planned a trip to Gettysburg with a tour guide. The homeschool students were put into two groups, representing the North and the South. Adam, my eldest son, got "elected" as the officer on one side.

The boys and I loved to bake when the kids were young. We baked, and they ate everything, especially desserts like funnel cakes. Once, Bryte accidentally used baking soda instead of baking powder in the funnel cake batter, and no one could eat it. So we threw it out and made another batter. The boys' favorite was making brownies and cookies. We made several different kinds of cookies, and I allowed them to lick the batter off the beaters. Somebody always got to lick the bowl, and the last one got a spoonful.

One time, the eldest sent me a Mother's Day card. It said, "A good mom lets me lick the beaters. But the best mom unplugs the beaters first."

I was always good at stretching the food budget. The boys thought I belonged to the "Turkey a Month" club because I baked a lot of turkeys. Pathmark, a grocery store, discounted them ten cents for each $10 purchase. If I purchased $50, I could buy a turkey for nineteen cents a pound. That's less than $3 for a fifteen-pound turkey! So I made turkey casseroles for them, and the leftovers sometimes went to a potluck group that appreciated them better. They often got tired of the cream of chicken soup in the crockpot and didn't want to look or eat it again. But they did like the turkey salad. I learned that they would eat that as many times as I would make it. To this day, I still enjoy creating meals with leftover turkeys. They visited a lady that she called herself "the squash lady." She grew a variety of squash and then made things with them. She inspired Adam to grow his squash, cut a hole, and plant a flower. It hung in his bedroom window!

We always had a live Christmas tree. There was a Christmas tree farm near us where we could get a ride in a wagon to drive to a location, get out, and then pick out our tree. When we bought it, they put plastic netting around it to keep it together and tied it to the car's hood.

We didn't have the money for a live tree for one year, so someone lent me a fake tree. But the boys refused to decorate it. It wasn't that large, and they were just so disappointed. They called it a Charlie Brown tree.

So, the following year, I had a part-time job selling computers at Circuit City and had to learn a new "language" there. I earned extra cash selling extended warranties for laptops. So that year, I bought a live Christmas tree, and the boys enjoyed the holidays like before, making cookies and helping me decorate them.

When I homeschooled, the boys had chores like helping to cook dinner and cleaning up afterward. Later, Bryte joined home ec classes. A few times, He even made dinner for us, like shepherd's pie and Mexican enchiladas, which took a lot of work.

Later, after homeschooling for three years, I added sales and tutoring jobs before substituting and later full-time work. I sold various products like *World Book Encyclopedias* (before the digital version), vitamins and nutrition, socks, and later computers. Then, soon after, I worked in customer service, selling lumber, tools, and plants at Home Depot. While at Home Depot, I received a call to interview to teach at Dickinson College. It was a small window, opened only for a semester. I taught "How to Teach Reading" to future teachers who would teach elementary students. Later, I secured a full-time job as a Management Assistant at the U.S. Army War College. That was a nice segue to honing my computer and work skills for my next job at ITT. There, I took advantage of getting another certification: ESL (English as a Second Language). The extra credits were necessary for me to re-enter the public school system full-time. I needed continuing education credits because of new laws that had been passed.

Finally, I secured a job teaching reading to adjudicated males in a locked-down facility an hour and a half away. It was a minor miracle that after thirty years, I would get back into the classroom to teach reading full-time and build upon my small pension. It was a great teaching job as I could create my own curriculum and worry less about paperwork such as lesson plans and parental conferences.

My students were the most challenging part due to their background of broken homes and criminal behavior. Being the only female teacher among them was difficult, as I became the scapegoat for all the misdeeds in our wing. I could take credit for a few, but I was the easy target and worked extra hard to defend myself—more on that later.

7

The Terrible Teen Years

Adam was a referee for boys soccer and later girls softball teams. He created hats on the sewing machine, which he sold to other teens. Bryte worked as a cashier at a local grocery store, while Chase worked at a local flower and garden shop and cleaned at the school during the summer. I was delighted to receive a flat of flowers and a nice flower pot for Mother's Day that year.

Earlier, their first job was to pick strawberries at a local farm. Adam would ride his bike a few miles one way there and back. Later, when Bryte joined him, I would drive them to work. Later, they would pick various vegetables. Adam worked at least ten years there and advanced to driving the truck to local grocery stores. He would learn to eat his lunch quickly to finish his route before the end of the day.

The worst thing about the job was their dirty

clothes. I had to soak them before I could even wash them. On days when they gathered eggs, their pants smelt awful! However, it was good, honest work that built discipline.

With three active teens, we could secure a young Christian couple to stay in our home while we went on a week-long Alaskan cruise to celebrate our 25th wedding anniversary! Adam was seventeen and a junior, Bryte was fifteen, a sophomore, and Chase was eleven in public schools.

It was rare to vacation on our own, but this was a unique opportunity as Chad had met Dr. Clyde Narramore, a Christian psychologist and best-selling author, on a plane ride, who then sent his monthly magazine. On the back cover, I discovered an Alaskan cruise to depart near the time of our special day. I had money for this vacation since I had a thriving nutrition business that year. Once we had our caregivers in place, we could relax and enjoy ourselves as it would be our last vacation together for quite a while. Little did we know how true that would be.

That week, Chase and his friend, Chris, decided to bike to Sheetz, a neighborhood gas station, for snacks. There were better ideas than this so late at night. First, there was no safe-lighted bike route at night, and secondly, there was a curfew. He was not even supposed to be at Chris's house overnight. Perhaps Chad permitted them when he called nightly. And we didn't know Chris's mom or how lax she was with rules and discipline.

Our teens got stopped by the police, as it was past curfew. A phone call to Chris's mom and our caregivers by the police to "Come get your teen" surprised everyone. We were alerted when Chad called home that night. Not a great end to our relaxing cruise! As a result, our caregivers also had to be strict with Bryte. He rebelled and locked himself in his room, and refused to cooperate. I can't remember many more details as time passed. I also lost track of the young couple who helped us, as they moved soon afterward. I sure hope our experience didn't deter them from having their children.

Though it wasn't that serious an infraction compared to what was to become the "Terrible Teen Years," it did usher in the challenge. "Gee, that was fun and exciting. What can we do next?" Thankfully for Chris and his older brother, they were rescued by Hershey's legacy. Let me explain.

Milton Hershey built a Foundation to house orphans and single-parent families (low-income) from youth to adulthood. This Foundation included a small house (rather than a dormitory) with house parents and private schooling. All expenses for clothing, room, board, and incidentals were included. With good grades and behavior, students could earn a college degree or trade school certification immediately after graduating with their high school diploma. Our neighbor was blessed to qualify for this program. Both sons got a college education and later good jobs.

God was good to provide us with a few "breaks" between crises. Family trips to Gettysburg, Pittsburgh, Tennessee, and the beach! Our boys loved any adventure with nature as well. Our last family vacation was to Niagara Falls before Adam left for college. Then we'd take short trips to visit him, especially the first year.

Once, I was talking on the phone, not paying attention to the speed limit while traveling locally through a known speed trap. Stopped. Yes, guilty with a ticket which I dutifully paid quietly. Next week, I'm driving with Chad to a favorite Mexican Restaurant. On the way back, we traveled through the same speed trap, and again, I was not paying attention to my speed. I got stopped!

"Please show me your license.".

"Yes, Officer."

"Oh. Are you Chase's mom?"

"Yes, sir," I replied.

"How's he doing?"

"He's on the football team and made the Honor Roll, sir!" I proudly announced. He returned to his car and undoubtedly noticed that I had been stopped just last week at this spot. He returned and said, "You've been through a lot. I'm just going to give you a warning this time." Hallelujah! Later, I told Chase, "Hey, it paid to be your Mom, jokingly… but I'm sure you still owe me."

Fast forward a few years. Our oldest son, Adam,

attended college in Tennessee, where fireworks are legal. Their dad saw an opportunity to purchase several for our boys' pleasure. Shortly afterward, Chase, the youngest son, and his best friend, Brad, were enjoying a "Big bang or two" in our backyard in the middle of the day. Unfortunately, the neighbor's elderly husband was resting, and she complained to the police about this disturbance. The boys were caught having lots of fun with "the evidence in hand." That was just the beginning of the next decade of trouble and hours of community service for Chase.

Each time, the crime and the hours seem to multiply exponentially. Seeking revenge, the boys retaliated by digging up an elderly couple's plants and decorating their garage door with catsup and eggs. Unfortunately, it was the wrong neighbor. This kind neighbor warned his dad first of the deed before calling the police, hoping he would take care of this before another incident happened.

"Oh, they were brown eggs," she added.

And that night, the boys woke up in the middle of the night to do more harm to the garden and decorate their garage door with brown eggs and more catsup. I was working late and didn't get the message in a timely manner. His dad would become paralyzed and just couldn't make a decision by himself. I knew we bought brown eggs locally, and he also knew. Chase was asleep while his dad waited for me to return home from work, or so he pretended, as we discovered later. I also noticed there was dirt under my son's fingernails. Though our son denied the deed, his friend confessed to his dad and added Chase's name as a co-conspirator.

That ended the friendship with Brad and his dad. We grieved the loss of the dad as well as Brad. Chase would do chores for the dad, who took him fishing and on camping trips. No more. That was a major turning point in our son's life and ours. Did Chase feel any remorse? Did he regret his friend's confession?

Consequently, lots of community service for the firework incident and destruction of the neighbor's property were just the beginning. He masked any disappointment of losing his friendship with Brad and his dad. He found acceptance with some troubled teens at school. Perhaps he felt like a hoodlum because he started to hang out with the wrong crowd in junior high.

I did pull Chase out of seventh grade and homeschooled him successfully that year. We could continue with one of the homeschool co-op groups and take field trips together. I attempted to rescue him, but I hadn't prepared him mentally for the change. He still gravitated to his old friends on weekends. He rebelled that summer and wouldn't cooperate another year.

Thinking back on events, I recall that Adam followed the rules and set a good example for his brothers and teens in the youth group. He even prayed for us daily. And that made a big difference in our lives.

Then, he went to college in Tennessee and got busy with school and life.

My prayers and faith got me through these following turbulent times. I planted a huge garden, one bed at a time. It was my therapy to play in the dirt and see herbs and flowers grow. But, before I could put a walkway to the backyard, Chase used it for a bike path and built a few humps to make it more exciting. After one of his infractions, I had him haul mushroom soil and spread it out as a punishment. Whew, did that stuff stink! I had several truckloads, but it's too bad I didn't use his help at the beginning. He did behave for a while after that job.

Another special time was when Adam brought his wife on Thanksgiving weekend. Together, we rode in a wagon and chose a Christmas tree at the Tree Farm. It was one of our few good memories. While decorating, I shared my ornaments and some Christmas decorations.

Now in eighth grade, Chase shared a locker with "Al." Al's brother had been on "house arrest" with an ankle bracelet. But that night, he got high on drugs and stabbed his mom, who died. He also injured his sister and her boyfriend, as well as Al. The brother then committed suicide. It was all over the news. Later, Chase visited Al in the hospital and gave him his winter coat as it had gotten colder. (These friends came from broken homes and already had bad reputations).

At the funeral of Al's brother, the school counselor

attended and observed that our son seemingly didn't belong with this group of "hoodlums." This was middle school and just the start of five more turbulent years. We later discovered our son had broken curfew, sneaking out late at night and returning many times while we were still asleep. (Our new bedroom was not adjacent to his). Later, alcohol and drugs were involved.

A well-meaning pastor advised us not to bring him to church as he was disruptive. It's too bad no other male leaders stepped up to the plate to mentor our son or walk alongside us. Who knows if it would have made a difference? Later, we were given court-ordered counseling for our son and us as parents. But we didn't have that opportunity for a mentor in church, our home, or our community. (I might look to mentor someone now.)

An earlier incident a few years prior to this may enlighten the reader regarding the discipline practice. While on a family vacation at the beach, our middle son, Bryte, threw a temper tantrum. He was angry and upset and refused to pack his suitcase when it was time to leave. He said he hadn't ridden on the go-carts or other rides yet. Oh, but that was last year when Uncle Wayne took our boys on rides while vacationing with his cousins. This time, it was only our family, and there wasn't extra money for rides. Rather than explain that to this son, who was usually obedient, Chad took off his leather belt. He began to whack his behind just as his dad would discipline him and his brothers.

"Stop!" I yelled as it was getting out of control: too long and too violent. He stopped, put away the belt, and never used the belt or any other form of discipline for any of the boys again. Chase was the one who needed more guidelines and more discipline. Yet, I believe this incident defined future discipline or lack of it. We could have benefited from more disciplined and consistent parenting skills.

When the boys were teenagers and had problems, we could not work together to solve them. We counseled with various ministers and counselors for twelve-plus years. It seemed to work for a time, but when situations happened that "didn't fit the mold," Chad forged his own path, saying the counselors just didn't understand or he'd just change counselors. It was totally frustrating for all of us.

I'd like to think that we did the best we could with the knowledge and experience we had at the time. Hindsight is clearer now. Perhaps, their dad froze at the moment, and instead of beating the boys, he did nothing. It was not the best alternative. I should have stepped up to the plate earlier, but at that point, Chase had no respect for any authority, and he was huge at this point. (He wasn't part of a gang, but he did have an allegiance of some sort to these friends).

Once, Chase and his friends went camping at a local state park. They arrived after a physical person-ranger had left to collect their fee, so they decided to skip it as if it didn't count. They disregarded putting the required overnight fee in the drop-box. They might have just gotten a warning in the morning, but they stayed up late and drank a few beers, leaving the evidence on the picnic table. They were carded: guilty! Our son was the only one under twenty-one and took the blame for the rest as he was still a juvenile. For this deed, he accumulated one thousand hours of community service. Fortunately, he could work at home helping with a newsletter for a non-profit organization (Bethesda Missions).

Ching! Ching! Now, Chase began to calculate how much money he could have earned if he were paid! And that was his last mistake! No, he didn't stop drinking or using drugs. No, his friends never volunteered to help him. But he did learn to be more discreet about his location. He chose a friend's house or our house when we were gone.

Imagine when Chase turned sixteen years old, he wanted his driver's license. He would be very cooperative and studious for a period of time. On the day of his test, he passed but got a ticket on the same day for not stopping at a stop sign near our home. I found the crumbled ticket in the trash. Later that year, he crashed his first car into a tree, and later, a second one was involved in a total collision. By the third car, he was "on his own" and bought a newer car that he seemingly took better care of. Surprise, he was growing up!

There is not enough paper to write of Chase's antics that would land him in the Alternative Education program in high school. Holes in walls and doors when our sons got angry. Vomit on the new rug because he wouldn't clean his friend's mess. Next time, candle wax. This was discovered when, at the last minute, he changed his mind about going with us for a weekend visit to see relatives. Then there were all the wonderful pets he nurtured: cockatiels, gerbils, a hamster, rabbits that multiplied when we vacationed, a ferret that made a tunnel in a couch, and a snake from a camping trip that delivered six babies.

We lived in a good neighborhood close enough to the high school so our boys could walk to school. Yet there were times when Bryte and Chase couldn't get there on time or at all. Chase made the honor roll in the first semester of his junior year (mostly A's, as I recall). So, in his mind, if he failed several classes, it would average to a "C," and he would pass. Unfortunately, there was also an attendance requirement, and he missed passing by .1 percentage points.

Consequently, he had to repeat his junior year. Chase was already older than most of his friends, as his birthday was in September. I did persuade his counselor to allow Chase to be recognized as a Senior in his last year playing football. Chad and I were also permitted to receive the honor of escorting Chase across the football field. (I was pleasantly surprised with a red rose to wear). One shiny memory amidst many large dark clouds.

The following year, Chase had some minor fractions and decided not to attend detention, resulting in him not crossing the stage to get his high school diploma. It wasn't important to him!

Fortunately, Chase compared notes with his friends and their families to see that college made a difference in their lifestyles. He was determined to attend Indiana University of Pennsylvania, a party school with an undetermined science major. Later, a professor recognized his potential and encouraged him to pursue a pre-med degree. His older brother, Adam, added that he needed to earn all A's to be accepted into graduate school. That worked!

He abstained from drugs to my knowledge. He did say he was offered pills but refused them. Another college friend and also his roommate left college because of a drug addiction. One family was able to afford rehab, and their son returned to school a year later. The other never returned.

That was just a glimpse of what we were dealing with our youngest son, who needed more guidelines, discipline, and rules enforcement. Often, he was so sneaky that he got away with much too late for us to discipline.

Meanwhile, if our lives weren't complicated enough, our middle son, Bryte, who had never given us problems, started to have a few issues in his senior year. He had been taking a particular prescription drug, Accutane, for his acne (not that it was really that bad, but the drug seemed to help. His complexion looked good). But the summer before his senior year, he discovered a zit on his face and got permission for an extra dose. Little did we know at the time that one side effect was depression (And as parents, we had to sign a waiver at the beginning to avoid bringing a charge against Hershey Medical Center).

Our first clue was when he had his senior pictures taken. He wore glasses (very recently) and didn't like his pictures. No problem. Let's get a retake, but then Bryte couldn't decide which ones he liked, so he paid for the whole package! He didn't even ask us! This was quite unusual because he was usually frugal with the money that he had earned. Later, we realized he was having difficulty making decisions (our first notable sign of depression).

"Dad, I want to quit school. It's just too hard. It's not fun," Bryte complained.

"What? Why?" his dad asked. He was encouraged to drop his part-time job instead. (If we had known that he didn't need all those credits, we could have had a conversation with his counselor.)

Each morning, Bryte would take a shower and get dressed for school but then lay back down on his bed and go to sleep. When he did go, he would often be late and then have to serve detention. After a few weeks of this behavior, I asked a counselor friend if our son could be depressed.

"Yes, try getting him to your family physician," he replied.

I tried. He was stubborn and uncooperative. When I managed to drive him, he wouldn't go into the office or budge from the car. (That would have been the best solution). I felt my hands were tied. So, this daily grind continued for another month or so.

Then, one late Sunday afternoon, Chad and I took a bike ride around the block for thirty minutes or so. When we returned, Chase, the youngest son, was locked in the upstairs bathroom. He then climbed out the window and had just escaped when we returned. We noticed a hammer in his belt. "What's going on?" we asked.

Chase explained, "I was making a sandwich to share, but Bryte wasn't happy. He said my half was bigger. Then he threw the (butter) knife at me and was so angry he grabbed Adam's juggling clubs and chased me. His eyes glared and actually scared me. I ran and hid in the bathroom." This was unusual for Chase, as he rarely refused any challenge.

"But Bryte came after me and clubbed the bathroom door, put huge gashes through the hollow door. Mom, he had this angry, frightening look in his eyes. I've never seen him like this before. I climbed out the window and jumped down. I grabbed a weapon from the garage in case he came again," Chase explained.

We then checked on Bryte, who was locked in his bedroom. "Bryte, open the door," demanded his dad. We could hear incoherent groaning sounds from inside. Dad got a tool to unlock the door. And there was our son in a fetal position, on the floor, making weird, strange sounds. Who was this person? (Our son was usually obedient, and he never got in trouble in school other than being tardy). He was the quiet one, not aggressive.

We called 911. About forty-five minutes later, the police arrived and handcuffed our honor student, who was still crumbled into a fetal position on the floor. If there were words to describe how this mother felt, that was like a gut-punch-heart-wrenching moment forever etched in my heart and mind. It was as if someone stuck a knife through my heart, twisted it, and pushed it deeper! It hurt beyond anything I could imagine.

Why the handcuffs? Was this protocol? He was not a threat at this point. Imagine how my son was feeling. Where was God in all this? There were no answers then or ever! But after consulting with a NAMI lawyer, that practice was changed. No more handcuffs.

This one incident would change our son's life, our lives, and our family's lives forever. The next few days, weeks, months, and years would be badly altered by that one phone call, police visit, and one set of handcuffs—the worst decision of our lives ever. Haunting thoughts of that decision reverberated in our minds still to this day. What else could we have done? Were there other options? Once a person is in "the system," it's difficult to reverse the path, as we were to find out.

Remember that we had our own baggage that we brought into our marriage, and when the problems came, we were "paralyzed!" Chad turned inward, isolating himself. (At least they didn't take either son to jail this time: just the psych ward at the hospital. But so many people don't understand mental illness, and there's a stigma attached to it. I had more understanding with all that I went through with my own mom. Yet, there was so much I didn't know). And some things I still don't understand!

At the hospital, our son, Bryte, stopped talking to anyone who was in authority. He would converse with other patients (and one young attendant whom he thought was just a visitor or patient). He was kept the minimum of three days, and then in the next rushed hearing, his stay was extended, even though Bryte hadn't talked. Hmm. He found out this second hearing was illegal and made a call to a lawyer. (As I write this, it seems so surreal. Yet here we were in the middle of this crisis with no apparent ending).

Another hearing, and this time, Bryte defended himself with words. (I took off work that Friday because I had to see and hear this! The extended stay was expunged from the record. We stopped at a restaurant on the way home to celebrate. Bryte couldn't decide what to eat—too many choices. His dad chose for him. Then Bryte decided he liked my dinner better and ate mine!

But that didn't mean things changed at home or school. He stopped talking to us – literally for years.

(Note: he did talk when he felt the need and to friends with whom he felt comfortable). He didn't do any work at school for a week or more. We learned later that a resting time for his mind and body was needed after his episode. His dad would now freeze when anything unusual happened. (Although he was caught conferring with his mother about our problems on the phone. I sensed the coolness in her demeanor toward me and Chase). Chad was afraid to make a decision about disciplining or following through in a counseling session, as we were court-ordered to do. Now, perhaps you can empathize with our problems. Big problems that wouldn't go away.

For the next eleven years, we would visit our son, Bryte, in various hospital stays. He stopped talking as if that was what got him in trouble. We would have to guess what he wanted to eat or where he wanted to go. One time, he needed a haircut, but by the time his dad figured that out, the barber shop at the mall had closed! That was before a holiday. The next day, we ended up taking him to a hotel restaurant for a nice dinner. I can imagine that some people may have surmised that we had treated a homeless guy.

When it was my turn to visit, I'd give him a pen and paper. "I give up. Write down where you want to go." And that worked for both of us. Playing mini golf, eating at local restaurants, and visiting a local fair to eat funnel cakes were fond memories.

The first long stay at the hospital included a transitional time where Bryte could come home for several hours on a Friday afternoon with his counselor/ case worker. I had to juggle my work schedule for these visits. Everyone in the office was surprised when I volunteered to work Saturday mornings, having Friday afternoons free. (No one wanted to work Saturdays). During his first longer stay, Bryte got behind in his computer classes. He could not finish those classes as he could not use a computer in the hospital. Healing took time. In addition, new meds or any meds didn't always agree with him. There were unpleasant side effects that would cause him to feel bad, so he neglected to take them shortly after he got home.

Sometime later, the cycle would begin again. He reacted in two specific ways. At times, he would get violent and destroy property, such as throwing large, heavy items. Lots of evidence: huge holes in walls and doors. (Years later, I was thankful that he never hurt us or anyone. I don't think I could forgive myself if I had to endure the pain of others as well). Other times, he would stop eating. This would go on for several days. Imagine a tall, strong teen not eating. Day after day, I would call the hospital emergency line.

"Can I bring him in today? It's been three days, four days...."

His body was so emaciated that after the emergency call was made, someone had to carry him on a stretcher down the steps. I didn't recognize this lean, skinny guy. It was scary! Yet, there were times when he would hide his dishes so well that we wouldn't know if he ate while we were working. It was an unsettling time to put it mildly.

Little did we know at the time that visiting various hospitals on holidays and special times of the year would become routine. It would be difficult to plan our lives as it revolved around these hospital visits. I tried to journal our experiences, but it seemed like a broken record. Over and over, the same scenario played. Would there ever be a breakthrough? Yet this was just the beginning of the next eleven years. Trauma surfaced on every holiday and even our anniversary. All ruined! The biggest hole in my wall was near the front door when a large, heavy speaker stack they used at band concerts was thrown down the steps to the first floor.

Perhaps that's why Adam and his wife stopped visiting as much. However, their visit was a welcome change for us. And there really wasn't one family member who understood or was willing to listen to discover what was going on. That was wisdom because they had no real solutions. Neither of us had the time to really share what was happening.

Were there alternatives? Yes, but once someone is in the public system of mental health or police system, it's difficult to get on another track unless you have a BIG bank account! We did find some answers about mental illness, its causes, medication, and how to talk with our son through NAMI (National Alliance of Mental Illness). They provided a local support group as well as educational classes. Chad and I took the classes, and I went a step further, taking training to become a teacher/facilitator and taught classes for a couple of years.

Having a support group of others who could empathize with us was encouraging. One woman, in particular, had such peace as she told her story about her son, even while she was still in the midst of it. That spoke volumes to me as I silently prayed to be more like her! (Be careful what you ask or pray for, because it took me years for that peace of mind and heart).

There were several more years of turmoil which included years of isolation from many friends who loved to visit, play games, and enjoy an evening of fun and food. During that period, it seemed I couldn't cover up the holes fast enough before another one surfaced. Holes in my home, my purse, and, more importantly, my heart!

There was another crisis that may explain why no one in my family in Pittsburgh was empathetic to me and my situation. Mom had a double stroke that fall. I believe it was during Bryte's senior year of high school. After her stay in the hospital, my younger sister, Carole, made a place for Mom in her home. She had promised Mom that she would care for her rather than put her in a nursing home.

While Carole worked full-time, she had a visiting nurse care for some of her needs. She learned to use a feeding tube and change her. During the day, her husband was available. Carole worked just five minutes away should she be needed to care for her. Mom's stroke left her unable to walk or talk. She communicated with her eyes or squeezed with her hand. We visited when we were able. My sister, Jan, would paint Mom's nails.

Meanwhile, during our crisis at home, valuable items disappeared… money, musical instruments, rings, and a watch from Chad's grandfather. Evidence that someone was stealing. Now we had to lock our bedroom doors and hide valuables as well. I hid extra money in the pockets of my clothes. That summer, when I wasn't able to work, there was always some money when I needed it. The supply lasted until my next job in the fall.

Once, while visiting Bryte at the hospital an hour and a half away, we got a phone call from Chase. The water was running in our bedroom bathroom and leaking through the floor. Our bedroom door was locked, and he couldn't get in. He just had to wait till we could return. What a mess!!

That summer, I volunteered to come to Pittsburgh as I was between jobs. The Holy Spirit told me Mom was dying and she needed me. (You might ask how he talked. It was an impression that I felt strongly. I knew I had to go and check on Mom and stay as long as needed). No one else in the family would notice yet.

I stopped at the hospital to visit and gave Mom a drink of water that was in a glass nearby. Little did I know that she couldn't swallow very easily. But a day later, Mom was released into Carole's care. Yet Hospice couldn't come as long as she was working full-time. Her husband was now staying in their cabin for the summer. So, I was needed to watch Mom during the day. I learned to use the feeding tube so I could give my sister a break one weekend.

Dad would visit daily for two hours, which gave me a break to spend time with my nieces. I took turns taking them shopping or just running errands. They called me the "bag lady" as I had so many extra shopping bags in my car. The first purchase was for rat poisoning, as I discovered some droppings in the basement where I was staying. So, a day later, I "bagged a mouse" as I caught him, put it in a double bag, and dumped him in the larger garbage bag. The "Bag Lady" to the rescue!

Though it was a relief from my personal crisis, I called home nightly to hear news of my family. I would hang up the phone and cry myself to sleep. Chad was seemingly paralyzed and unable to carry out discipline. After a month of living with Dad one night and my sister the next night, I called Aunt Marge, who invited me to stay with her and Uncle Roy. The peace, quiet, and loving nature of Aunt Marge gave me the strength to continue.

Our family had gathered around Mom earlier in the week, with my brother (in Tennessee) on the phone. We expressed our love, said our goodbyes, and gave her permission to leave us for Heaven. But she stayed a while longer to have the Pastor visit. She had taken no food the last couple of days as her body was shutting down. We knew the end was soon.

The next Sunday was the Faust Reunion. Dad came early to visit Mom and left to entertain his relatives with his music at the reunion. On my way home from church, I got the phone call: Mom is having trouble breathing. Hurry if you want to talk to her. I came back to reiterate my love and to see Mom's last breath! I was glad I did.

My sisters and I had decided we couldn't go to the reunion and enjoy ourselves, so we stayed with Mom and had no regrets. The hospice lady was there and accompanied me to the Reunion, which was forty-five minutes away. We stopped at a grocery store to make a quick rest stop. I noticed some "Heart pins with names," and I chose three Dorothy Hearts for three sisters. (That was Mom's name). Thank you, Lord, for little things.

I was the one who told Dad that Mom was gone. He cried… the first time I remember my dad showing such emotion for Mom. He said, "I know she is with the LORD as she was a good wife and mother." And that's why he chose to stay with his relatives that day rather than return with us.

Before we prepared for Mom's funeral, my sister and I tried to have a day of fun when my brother visited. I remember going to the IKEA Store. I can't remember if we bought anything there. I just remember putting the shopping cart back, but since it was not secured on the hill, it started rolling back in my direction as it was "chasing me down." We laugh every time we think of that.

My husband and sons came later to pay their respects at the funeral. Each grandson shared how they thought they were Grandma's favorite. She really did love them all. Lord, help me to be as loving and forgiving as my mom was. No one can recall a bad comment that she made. On the day of the funeral service, I took refuge in a small room to review my notes. While there, I noticed a few cobwebs in the corner and laughed. Mom called them "boyfriends." And no "boyfriends" were allowed in our house! Thanks, Mom, I needed some comic relief! She was truly special and loved by all.

Dad would live about twelve more years. He stayed in his home until his dog, Lucky, died. Then he moved into the apartment under the office where he had his insurance business with my sister, Carole. Later, he was diagnosed with cancer, and the doctor nicked his "bladder," leaving him with an urgency to be near the bathroom within an hour after eating a meal.

The steps inside leading to the basement and outside steps behind the building became an obstacle then. He also had a loss of his eyesight shortly after eye surgery and had become cancer-free. (He was legally blind, seeing only shadows. He purchased a special machine to magnify print when he needed to read documents).

Dad's brother, Ray, who lived nearby, would take him grocery shopping on Thursdays and help him read the labels. Dad hated to give up driving, but with limited sight and a good memory, he still knew the streets. Sometimes, Dad would take the bus or accept rides from strangers on rainy days. I cautioned him as that wasn't safe. Oh, he was convinced he could easily escape out the car door.

"Not if they locked the doors! And if they don't kill you, they could injure you badly," I added. I think I finally scared him into no longer accepting rides from strangers. He would often give some poor stranger money, who then noticed where he lived. Carole, sitting near the front door, had to turn them away.

Dad refused to go to a nursing home as long as Carole, our youngest sister, could help with meals, laundry, and his bills. She paid all his bills, but he gave away most of his Social Security checks to Pastor Bob and other charities. He lived simply and invested his earnings wisely when he worked.

After falling too many times, Dad finally agreed that he would go to a nursing home. My brother and sisters and I visited several homes to decide where he should go. Meanwhile, SM, my new husband, asked Dad where he would like to go. Dad said he wanted to go to Tennessee to live with Wayne. Wayne was okay with that but needed a little time to prepare. We agreed to have Dad stay at a nice nursing home for one month. It was close to both sisters in Pittsburgh. Then, Dad would travel to Tennessee. I don't think Dad believed us, or perhaps a month seemed like a long time.

Again, I said to SM, my husband, after a few weeks had passed, "I need to go to Pittsburgh. This time, my dad needs me." He was very depressed and had been staying in his room even when my sisters or Pastor Bob visited. I gathered his poetry and spent hours reading to him. As I read his poetry, tears streamed down his cheeks. It was healing tears. Though the nurses told me Dad was giving up and he wanted to die, I refused to believe it.

"It's not much longer," I encouraged Dad. "You will move to be with Wayne." I bought Dad some sweatpants as he had lost so much weight his pants wouldn't stay up. Again, we joined Dad for dinner and assured him it wouldn't be long before he'd go to Tennessee with Wayne. This time, he believed me!

At some point, Dad had to stay in an Assisted Living Home in Tennessee due to his incontinence. It was a nice facility, and he particularly enjoyed the other guests and the staff. Wayne visited Dad for two hours almost daily. If he had to miss a day, Dad would get a little depressed and pout. Jan, our middle sister, would also visit on her way to Florida. I came and helped Dad get settled the first week and several times during that year.

Dad had a brain hemorrhage and died peacefully. Wayne had to make all the arrangements to prepare his body in Tennessee and transport his body to Pittsburgh where he was buried. Thankfully, Wayne was better at paperwork than me! It was a lot, and I would have drowned in paperwork for decades with my ADD (distractions).

***

Things I Learned
From My Sons
(Sometimes the Hard Way)

1. I'm watching you! If it's different, I'll do as you do rather than what you say.

2. Spending time with me is more important than spending money on me (especially in their younger years. Go to the park, playground, nature trail, or the beach.

3. Try to "like" my friends or at least treat them respectfully. Feed us at home, and we'll stick around. (Watch them and get to know their friends).

4. As we reach our teenage years, we'd like to include our friends on our outings.

5. Allow me to grow up and mature. Don't do everything for me. Give me guidelines with time, money, and responsibilities.

6. Listen. I'm learning and growing and have opinions that may or may not agree with you: let me express them. (Set that atmosphere)

Mom's Add-Ons

1. Don't compare our abilities with our siblings (and if they're twins or close in age, give each their own time and gifts).
2. If there's a middle child, ensure he doesn't get "lost" in everyday life. He may need extra attention. Find his special interests.
3. Surprises are nice, but another sibling needed structure, while the other two enjoyed my spontaneity.
4. Support their teachers, preachers, and those in authority (though in this current age, know what's being taught. Be vigilant. Volunteer at church or in your community).
5. Forgive one another. And learn to for-

give yourself. Forgive me, your mom: I did the best I knew then!

6. Be Firm. Be consistent. Be fair with all your children. Rules and boundaries are crucial, as well as appropriate consequences. (Yelling and raising your voice is not always necessary). Magic 1, 2, 3 ...You give three warnings and then the consequence.

7. Each child is unique with their own love language (according to Gary Smalley's Five Love Languages). Find out which one speaks "I care..."

    - Affirmation and praise
    - Quality time spent together
    - Gifts or tangible things (need not be expensive)
    - Affection (hugs and kisses)
    - Touch (pats, fist bumps, wrestling, etc.)

In him we have redemption through his blood,
the forgiveness of sins, in accordance with the
riches of God's grace that he lavished on us.
With all wisdom and understanding,

EPHESIANS 1:7-8 (NIV)

PART IV

Broken Karen

SEPARATION & DIVORCE

8

Caged Rabbit

No one expects to be married for almost forty years only to give up at the end, but we had been building up to it for a long while with little to no communication and no shared goals. We both had baggage from childhood and families that we carried into our own family. After more than twelve years of counseling (we had been court-mandated to take counseling for Chase's misdeeds and for our lack of parental skills), there were no lasting changes. If Chad disagreed with a counselor's recommendations, we would change counselors. If a new crisis arose between us, it became another excuse to change counselors. At one point, I secured counseling for myself apart from Chad.

In addition to counseling, there were a few times when I would spend a night or two with a friend just to get some distance and relief from Chad. He would eventually call the house where I was staying and beg my friend to send me home. Once, I spent an entire week with a couple from my church without Chad knowing my whereabouts. I would talk with him over the phone, but I only ever saw him after I returned at the end of the week to attend my family reunion in Pittsburgh. By the way, no one at the reunion knew about our short separations. Probably because they were too distracted with their own relationship and health problems.

Desperate to save our marriage, Chad finally agreed to participate in a weekend marriage retreat with a local counselor and a minister from our church. It was an intense weekend that included small and large group sharing. Overall, it was refreshing and encouraging to both of us. However, all was forgotten when our next crisis arose two weeks later. We decided to attend a second follow-up weekend at the marriage retreat. Still, it ended up being traumatic for me. Chad violated one of the rules and disrespected me. Even though I didn't respond very well to his treatment, I was willing to share both of our sides during a counseling session at the retreat. Chad gave up on that group, but I participated in a third session as training to help with another class.

I am not sure of the timeline, but I finally felt the need to confide in Chad about the childhood sexual abuse I experienced. At the time, he was sympathetic and seemed to realize that I had dealt with those experiences that were a part of my past. But shortly after that, Chad threw it up in my face during another crisis. One reason I remember that so vividly is that it was Christmas Day. We had made plans to visit friends later that day. Instead, I packed a suitcase and told Chad I would stay with them for a few days. That Christmas marked the beginning of the end of our marriage.

I probably relived that incident in my head hundreds of times. How could Chad be so cruel as to blame me for the abuse and to dishonor me as if it were my fault? After a few days of my absence, he begged my friend to send me home, which she did—but only reluctantly. I was even more reluctant than her to leave and return home, and home was never the same. Just as I was plotting to go again, but for a more extended period, I lost my job and fell into a depression. My open door to leave had shut.

Meanwhile, life continued while I fought depression and the injustice of being unfairly terminated from my job. As low a point as that was in my life, however, I never gave up believing that God loved me. Part of my faith practice at the time was to pray for others. Sometimes, it was in a small group. Other times, I did it privately (I also began praying for my state of Pennsylvania and our nation). So, when asked by a friend to join her and a group to pray, I agreed. At the end of the prayer session, our hostess invited all who wanted personal prayer to come upstairs while the others could leave. I stayed and asked for prayer for my marriage and family. At the end of this personal prayer, the hostess offered her place as a refuge, should I need it.

"Thanks," I responded. "Please give me your contact information." She did, and I learned that she had already rescued several women and helped to restore their marriages.

A few weeks later, our family's pet rabbit died. He had been left in his cage with little food. While we were gone, a neighbor tried to give him lettuce, but the rabbit didn't survive. When I saw our pet lying still on the floor of his cage, it was as if the floor gave out underneath me. I felt like that rabbit in a cage: boxed in with no real life—just surviving day by day. What a wake-up call for me!

We had just returned from a weekend with Adam as he defended his doctoral dissertation. It was the July 4th weekend, and we had planned to see the fireworks at our church. The laundry wasn't done in enough time for us to leave together, so Chad left before I did. Chad had specific expectations about the laundry. All clothes had to be removed immediately after a load was finished. Then they had to be put in the dryer (the shirts had to be put on hangers). Chad also had specific rules for washing dishes. But the rules were for me and not my boys when it was all said and done. While Chad would try to enforce the rules with me, he didn't enforce the rules for the boys. Because the boys had no consequences for breaking the rules, they had no incentive to follow them. It was frustrating because I saw that I could be controlled and had willingly allowed it for decades. Shortly afterward, we had a heated discussion. Even though it was fifteen years ago, I still remember the yelling and name-calling through the closed bathroom door. But then, I made up my mind: I was done. I didn't want to continue feeling like a caged rabbit. I was dead inside, and I needed a permanent change.

I had waited for Chase to finish high school before I left Chad. Chase had just completed his first year in college with all A's, thanks to the encouragement of his older brother. As a reward, he went on a college trip to Costa Rica for two weeks (one week was community service, and the second was fun). I said goodbye to Chase a few days early as I put my suitcase in the trunk of my car before work, hoping to contact the hostess of the prayer group I previously attended.

Chase ended up not returning after two weeks. The owner of the animal refuge park where he was volunteering arranged for him to obtain his visa. Chase then began working for room and board (including someone to cook and do his laundry). Initially, he worked with the animals. Later, the owner secured a contract with a cruise company from California for Chase to tour his facility. Chase was able to earn tips from tourists. Chase was popular, speaking good English and learning Spanish later. With the tip money he made, he purchased a bike and would ride into town, where he hired a Spanish tutor and got beer. Chad visited Chase in the late summer. My sister and her son visited him as well.

Just as I had gotten a ticket to see him, Chase came home before Thanksgiving without notice. Having been away for that long, he had missed a semester at school. Dad ended up paying his student loan.

My first trip abroad on my own was to Chile during Chase's holiday break. It was a late airplane flight. After I fell asleep, my flight was changed to a different gate when I woke up. I was just so glad that I got there. I didn't even have a cell phone with any activation in a foreign country, nor the contact information of the person Chase was staying with. What was I thinking? I needed Chase to be dependable this time. He had better be meeting me there! I didn't know the language and was only a tourist. But thank God that he did meet me.

I visited Chase in Chile during his Christmas break. He was as happy to see me as I was to see him. I also needed him because I knew nothing about Costa Rica, especially the language. Chase was also glad to see me for another reason: he needed extra money. He grabbed the money from the ATM before I could even reach for it (no change there).

At the time, that's the way it was. He would ask for money from me for a specific purchase, and I helped him several times.

Nevertheless, I enjoyed my trip, though I only spent a little time with Chase. He spent time with his beautiful *senorita* (girlfriend). We attempted to take a small trip north to visit a beach resort. Of course, I paid for all expenses, though he and I never got to relax on the beach. Even though we arrived late, he enjoyed a few nice meals. But he was anxious to get back.

Our hostess was named "Cookie" and her family was hospitable. I enjoyed playing Dominoes with her, and we enjoyed each other's company even though we didn't know each other's language. I had the unique experience of going to the hairdresser with her in the middle of the day. I can't believe I had my hair colored in a foreign country—instead of a haircut! Fortunately, I liked the color (my only choices were dark or light blonde, which we bought in a separate shop). I guess that I feared someone would cut my long hair too short!

Because it was a holiday weekend, Cookie had a couple of other visitors for a few days. One was a doctor. After his girlfriend left, he massaged my feet and danced with me on the rooftop patio. I felt awkward and had no interest (he told me I had no rhythm. A year later, I took dance lessons repeatedly until I could feel the beat).

Upon returning, I worked in solitude while Chad continued to visit his senorita monthly for years as our divorce dragged on. Before Chad could marry his girlfriend, both sons talked with their dad and told him they didn't want him to marry her (thinking he would move to Chile). He did break it off and met his present wife shortly before our divorce was finalized. The boys were much happier with his new wife than with his girlfriend.

When Chase returned from Chile, he had no cell phone. Somehow, he lost it. Yet he still was able to contact me when he needed money. It's not that I was making a lot of money (a fraction of what his dad made). He needed a car. Still, I felt obligated to help because we had bought Adam a car during his senior year of high school. His dad had been paying for college, so I offered to loan him money to buy a used car. Of course, Chase wanted a loan that was more than I suggested, and I relented. Well, it was supposed to be a loan, but he never made a single payment (that was his plan). He had a habit of being friendly to me when he needed money. I was just happy to see him and help him.

One day, I visited Chase and saw he had a new iPhone but hadn't even attempted to pay me. I raised my voice at him in anger. Well, that didn't work. When he graduated from college, I gave him a lovely card and a note telling him I was proud of him and that my gift was his car. Did he appreciate it? I doubt he knew how long it had taken me to earn the loan amount (he crashed that car, too!) Later, he bought a newer Honda and took better care of it.

Chase completed his bachelor's degree in pre-med with all A's, honors, and many accolades. He was accepted into the doctoral program to study pharmaceutical medicine, which is actually more difficult than being accepted as a doctor of practicing medicine. But he had all A's, had studied abroad, and had also learned another language! I was very proud of him.

He continued to pursue a Doctorate in Pharmacy with Honors. Before landing a job in Florida, I attempted to visit him at his dad's place, where he was biding his time until he completed his tests for certification in Florida.

When I arrived, I knocked on the door.

"Hey, Chase. I just want to talk with you." But as he closed the door and window, he yelled, "I don't want to talk with you." I turned and left. It has been a while since I've spoken to Chase or seen him, but I heard he has settled down with a good job. I also heard through someone else that Chase has met the love of his life and bought a house. He's much more responsible now. He hasn't kept close contact with his brother either. The girls visited and saw his pet collection, but not recently. I guess he doesn't need money now.

This realization hit me so sad because I eventually found someone special who would love and cherish me—and was fluent in Spanish! I already had lost one son, and now essentially two sons. The third son is still a work in progress, as I would love to be with him more often.

I once enjoyed three sons, two granddaughters, and their mom. I am now nine miles from this last son and his family, but I see them briefly. Holidays can be lonely when not shared with relatives. At least SM's daughter visits and welcomes us at her home. We see her and his grandchildren a couple of times a year.

***

Dance of Praise

November 1, 2001

Lord, I've not got it all together right now: my life and family. We're all messed up. Is it okay to raise my hands and praise you even in my brokenness?

What will others think if they know how imperfect I am: how I failed as a wife and mother? My family, life, and world are seemingly falling apart. Will they think I am a hypocrite? I don't want to be a stumbling block.

Then, the following encouragement came from a friend: "Yes, you can worship the LORD in your brokenness. Let your praise minister to Him."

LORD, I bring to you my broken life. I offer you a sacrifice of praise. A sacrifice because I don't feel happy, jolly, or full of praise. But I choose to praise You and worship You because You are worthy. You are close to the brokenhearted, and that's me right now.

When I am brokenhearted, my worship and praise are like cinnamon sticks that are most fragrant when broken. Even the angels, in all their splendor, cannot sing such a melody. Lord, I pray that others may see Jesus is my strength. He is the reason I can praise. He is my partner in this dance of worship.

And then I heard Him say, *Yes, my daughter, let's dance.*

I will extol the LORD at all times.
His praise will always be on my lips.
Glorify the LORD with me.
Let us exalt his name together.

Psalms 34:1.3

Year's End

Another year has hurried to its end
And I've enjoyed the moment of each day.
I cherish time I spent with every friend
Both new and old I met along the way.
So, ring the New Year in with expectations
Of love, joy, peace and good health too,
And look ahead with great anticipation
That God is always smiling down on you!

Robert E Faust (my dad)

May the favor of the Lord our God rest on us;
establish the work of our hands for us—
yes, establish the work of our hands.

PSALM 90:17 (NIV)

PART V

Karen Unchained

RESTORATION

9

Single to Married Again

"Sometimes the grass looks greener on the other side (the neighbor's lawn)" is a cliché that says everyone else has it better or easier than we do. But a wise man once said, "If you take care of your own lawn, it will look great too!"

After two years of separation and divorce lawyers, Chad and I thought we were legally divorced and took off our wedding rings. To celebrate, I went whitewater rafting with a church singles group. It was a camping trip with catered food, but it was worth it!

I attended many singles events, but I was just looking for activities. My friend Becky organized a barn party with live music and a potluck for the second event. There were weekend trips to various state parks, and everyone contributed to the meals. Many were looking for a mate, and the "gene pool" looked like leftovers!

Next, I tried the dance events. However, I was turned off when one guy said he was sitting that dance out and then chose a different partner moments later. That's when I decided to try the dance clubs where everyone wanted to dance, even with beginners. As a bonus, there were swing dance lessons at the beginning. I found another dance hall in a college town near me. The young guys were old enough to be my son, but they still danced with me when I asked them. Some even asked me! (especially as I improved)

I enjoyed dancing on Wednesday nights after work, as it helped me release work stress and was a great exercise. I'd change my outfit at work and go directly to the dance club in downtown Harrisburg. The added benefit to these activities was that I was not limited to only internet dating.

I had tried a few dating sites but found all the scam artists instead. After conversing online for a month, I was ready to meet the first guy, Roger. The dating website said he was from Florida, but he was really from Africa. Just days before arriving at the airport, he called to tell me there was a problem. To get through customs, he wanted one thousand dollars. I had just returned to college for another certification to get back into teaching. It didn't feel right that he should be asking me for money.

"No, Roger, I can't help you." The end.

Then, another single guy with a son lived in Bowmansdale, a small town near me (I do not think you could even call it a town, but it did have a post office). I asked him a few questions about his son and offered some advice. That's laughable now as I write this. There was no son. He asked me to accept a package in the mail. Who knows what might have been in it? I ended that one quickly and reported him (like I reported Roger).

Finally, I found a date who really was local, so we met for dinner. A dear friend said I should give this guy (Bill) seven dates. So, I did. Bill had some baggage with two adult children living with him. One was on drugs, trying to recover. He also had another roommate who got sick and was sent to the hospital. I told Bill to pray The Sinner's Prayer with him or invite a pastor to pray. Bill chose the latter, and the guy accepted Jesus as his Savior! Shortly after Valentines Dinner at a local church, I clearly heard the LORD say to my spirit, "He's not the ONE!" It broke my heart to tell him and let him go.

Not long after that, a few guys from my Singles Bible Study Class introduced me to ballroom dancing. Again, there were group lessons at the beginning, which I took. Ballroom dancing includes so many dance variations and complicated steps. One guy friend, Steve, danced with me and taught me the basic steps. After that, it was time for private lessons. Cheri and I shared a private lesson with Stacey, our teacher. Oh, we laughed and had fun together! And dance lessons paid off. Less than a year later, we met our future husbands. My soon-to-be husband, SM, and I took more lessons together and enjoyed dancing everywhere there was music!

I wasn't in a hurry to get married. I did ask several prayer partners to meet SM before anything got serious. First, SM had to meet several friends at a dance (not a date). He passed the first test. Marilyn told her friends that he was a perfect gentleman. Then, I introduced him to others at my church, as he started to attend with me. Lastly, he met one of my pastors during a counseling session. The pastor's stern words still vibrate in my mind.

"Karen is one of our family, and you must never hurt her," he said. SM assured him that his intentions were honorable! Both were so sweet!

My son Adam and his wife gave me a game about life goals. The questions seemed quite personal yet serious, so I only played it once with SM. At the end of the game, each person was to read their life goal that they had written at the beginning. Mine was immediate.

"To finish my ESL certification and return to a teaching job for a better retirement."

Surprisingly, SM's goal was "to meet my life partner and share life's adventures together." I wasn't there yet! But he was patient and waited until I was sure I knew he was the one. Meanwhile, we enjoyed dinner, dancing, concerts, plays, and (retired professional) pinochle club.

When he invited me to his pool tournament, I surmised that his friends were older than me. I tried to look up his information online (including his age) to no avail. I only knew his nickname, but not his legal one. By the time I did find out, it didn't matter so much. Mandy, our ballroom teacher, said, "He's retired, so he'll have more time for you."

Eventually, I got my ESL (English as a Second Language) certification. I landed a job working with incarcerated males in a facility seventy-five miles away from where I lived. I calculated that I had to work four years to get a better partial pension when I retired.

Shortly after the divorce and before school started again, SM and I married, and I finally shared his home. He introduced me to the world of traveling when I retired a couple of years later. We were able to travel to many places around the world. It was exciting to see tourist attractions, but it was also exciting to see how people live in different parts of the world and experience new foods. My life has been enriched in many ways: first time for a garage door opener, a garbage disposal, and a full social calendar. Happily, I have a garage for my car again!

It hasn't been easy with a blended family at times. There have been many challenges. One was moving to another state and having to make new friends. Sometimes, we are the only ones we can count on. We joined a local church and were baptized in the ocean, which was a big highlight for me! I had been sprinkled as an infant, baptized in the river in my teens, and now in the ocean in my Golden Years!

We have since joined the Krewe, an organization that supports the military at parades on Veterans Day, Christmas, and Mardi Gras. Because my husband is an Air Force veteran of twenty-two years, we fit into this group well. We found a few bridge clubs and a few places to dance. We keep busy by volunteering at a local thrift store and church activities. Living close to the Pensacola Naval Air Station, we avail ourselves of the gym, kayaking, Chief's Club, and a private beach. We are also close to Alabama and have seen several plays and other live shows. We enjoy time with neighbors at the pool. Life happily goes on.

***

Santiago

November 9, 2015

God's Answer to Prayer for Me
Everything he needed to be.
Strong, confident, friendly,
A good dancer with a heart of gold.
Good-looking, fun-loving
With lots of stories to be told.
A confidant, a companion

A world traveler on time.
He's my someone special
To celebrate life in our new prime.
Laughing, sharing, playing games and cards.
Cooking and grilling in our backyard.
Entertaining others in our home.
Seeing sites in states and countries, we roam.
My friend, my lover, my partner in crime,
Yesterday, today, till the end of time.

***

Lessons *From My Dog*

1. When loved ones come to the door, run and greet them!

2. Delight in the simple joys of a walk. A bone for my dog as a treat of chocolate for me.

3. Naps are good! Stretch before rising.

4. Run, romp, and play daily!

5. When you are happy, dance around and show it!

6. Turn your face to the wind and feel the

breeze (with the car window down). For me, that means embracing the task head-on. The breeze, like peace, will come when it's complete.

7. Savor the moment! Be in the next moment. Enjoy the people and your surroundings!

8. On a hot day, drink lots of water and relax under a tree!

9. When it's in your best interest, practice obedience. (For me, it's doing the right thing).

In addition, people should always kiss before they leave one another and go to bed. You never know if it's your last, so make your last words gentle, kind, and positive.

***

Nine

Near-Death Experiences

1. In my teens, I experienced my first allergy attack. Though I got treatment immediately, it was only temporary. I had four more attacks over the next five years. By then, I was married, and the

emergency doctor said that my body couldn't take much more. I went to a specialist, only to discover I was now allergic to everything breathable: pollens, cats, dogs, molds, mildew, etc. There was no way to avoid all of them, so I took three allergy shots with three allergens in each. I took them for about eight years until I had a baby and prayed for healing.

"LORD, I can't do this anymore. Heal me!"

2. Before I got married, my brother's friend, Jack, had to navigate several swerving curves through the snowy mountain roads on my way home to see my brother before he left for Vietnam. The car slid, but Jack was able to maintain control. Winter in Pennsylvania could be scary.

3. Once, when Chad fell asleep on a turnpike, I believe an angel protected us, waking him up as our car careened against the middle guardrail. We all woke up. Thankfully, nobody was injured.

4. I had my first C-section in my twenties. Then, I had another C-section. Shortly after giving birth to my third son (a natural birth), I lost four units of blood. That's a lot, and the machines were down, so no one knew exactly what had happened. I asked Chad to call the prayer chain to ask the ladies to pray. They did, and I survived! God saw me through another crisis!

5. When I was President of CWA in my thirties, I had an asthma attack (perhaps related to stopping the allergy shots five years prior). Although I had an inhaler, I struggled that night to breathe. Chad and I stayed up all night and prayed. In the morning, I went to my doctor, who chastised me for not seeking help the night before. "You could have died," she reprimanded. "I've seen it happen."

6. Also, in my thirties, I ran over my own legs with my own car in my own driveway! It happened on a Wednesday night after church when I pulled our station wagon (three tons) up to the garage door and left the motor running. My two young sons were buckled in the front seat (no car seats back then). Their favorite antic was to turn the auxiliaries on (windshield wipers, radio, and heater). When I started the car, I would be startled, and they would laugh (me too). That didn't happen this time. They actually hit the gear shift, and the car shifted into neutral. With the door ajar, I attempted to get in the car to stop it from drifting down our sloped driveway onto the street and up the next driveway. Unfortunately for me, the car door knocked me down, and the front tire crushed my left leg five inches above my ankle and nine inches above my right ankle. Fortunately, the boys stayed in the car throughout the entire ordeal. After being run over, I walked in my stocking feet across the street to the car, opened the door, told the boys to get help, and then lay down until help

came. A neighbor saw it all and called 911. The EMT who arrived later told me, "A few more inches on the right leg, and it would have hit a major artery. You would be dead!" I never lost consciousness or broke any bones! And I still have a small indent in my left leg and dark veins in my right leg. Later, minor surgery helped reduce vein scarring.

7. In my forties, I was on my way to work when I hit black ice. I had driven up a hill. When I began to come down the hill, my car spun on a large patch of ice, doing a 160-degree-wide turn into a cornfield after knocking down a telephone pole. Emergency lights and screeching sounds from my car woke the family across the street. The young boy thought it was time to get up, but Mom knew it was another car accident and dialed 911. The first to arrive were firefighters and emergency workers who kept me calm. My sunroof was demolished, and glass had perforated my hat. I also had shards from my eyeglasses in my eyes that came out later when I cried. The front door was crushed and dented two feet deep by the impact of the telephone pole. I was considered a "borderline crisis." However, because of the car's condition, they decided to life-flight me to Hershey Medical Center. (I hesitated to have them call Chad because he had a late night watching a big Penn State Game). They made my car a convertible by cutting the top off to extract me. I might have injured my back. Later, after being thoroughly examined, I was

released.

8. In my sixties, SM and I had been vacationing in Yellowstone Park and were going to the airport one morning at 4:00 a.m. The only lights on the road were the ones on our van. I turned to my husband and said, "Let's pray." Then he asked me to look for deer as he looked to the right. I looked to the left. Three deer attempted to cross our path from the left side of the road just minutes after we finished praying. I gently put my hand on SM's arm, squeezed it, and said, "Slow down." (The speed limit was 80 miles an hour). The deer stopped and changed directions. Moments later, two more deer attempted to cross from the right side, but they also paused as we drove past. (Imagine a car accident with a rental car in the middle of nowhere. We would have missed our flight had we survived a crash). For the record, let's just say many circumstances were thwarted by the Holy Spirit's protection.

9. We were warned not to touch the monkeys while traveling in Gibraltar. At the time, it seemed harmless until a stranger standing near me slapped a monkey on its rear and then ran away. The monkey snarled at me and jumped in my direction. I quickly jumped and ran away. Okay, maybe that wasn't a near-death experience, but there are at least eight. Now I will be extra careful of my driving and yours should I let you drive!

Because I didn't have much fun in my childhood, I now have a lot of time to explore as many adventures as possible. So, pop the popcorn and turn on the music: I am ready to party, dance, and have fun!

That's my new script: "This too shall pass!" Don't sweat the faults and misdeeds of others. They probably meant no harm.

Some of my dearest friends have seen me grow through trials and sorrows. We have shared many tears, prayers, and encouraging words with a cup of coffee or tea with a homemade salad. We have also stayed in touch even though I moved many miles away. We share happy times and difficult times when we need prayers. Carol M sent a prayer via a text (instead of just saying, "I'll pray"). It touched my heart, and I now send others encouraging prayers. Many friends have begun to send prayers to others as well! Carol M is one of those "gold friends" I will answer the phone for no matter how busy I am. I will pray immediately when I hear of her or her family's needs. I am confident she still does the same for me. We have known each other for over thirty years, homeschooling and spending time together. We have so many good memories. I could always count on Joyce and Carol H, who have known me for years, to pray as well.

***

Hats, Hats, Hats!

When nothing else fits, a hat always does, adding a little height to me! (5'1")

Bright clothes and later accessories too. I wanted to stand out in the crowd!

As Catholics, we wore hats to church, especially on Easter, as we were to cover our heads. A small handkerchief folded in a triangle would suffice as a covering at other times.

As a teen, I saved my babysitting money to purchase a hat for Easter. Just as I had saved enough, a missionary came to our Protestant church, and I felt the need to surrender my hat money in the offering plate to help someone who needed it more than I did. Fast forward years later, and I have six hats. I lent them to a woman from church for a display, but she ruined a few when she set them in the window of her mobile home. The sun had faded them, though she never noticed. But later, I was blessed to find a few good bargains and was given some as well. I refreshed the older hats with new ribbons and braided bands.

At one point, I counted sixty hats. There were not enough Sundays in a year to wear them all, so I wore them often, anywhere, and anytime. People can identify me just by my hats. Once, a lady in a local movie theater said, "Oh, you're the hat lady from church," though she didn't know my name. And in a crowded parking lot at Hershey Stadium, I heard someone yell, "Hey, Karen! Hey, hat lady!" It was my signature for years.

It was Easter Sunday, and since Adam's first degree was in ministry, we visited the church where he worked.

"Mom, you may not want to wear a hat today as it's a small country church, and you will probably be the only one wearing a hat." Hmm, I couldn't make up my mind whether I should or not, so I just took it with me. When we entered the small parking lot, I said, "Adam, I'm going to wear a hat anyway. It's okay if I'm the only one." So, I did. At the end of the nice service, a stranger came up to me and said, "You are an answer to prayer."

I looked at him with a puzzled expression on my face. He added, "I told the LORD that if I had to wear a tie, there better be a lady wearing a hat." I smiled as I was speechless, which doesn't happen often (just ask my sons, friends, or husband).

When I moved from Pennsylvania to Florida, I sold a few but gave many away, along with the hat boxes. One special memory was Tess's picture of her two little granddaughters wearing my hats! How precious. Sometimes, I just have to let things go.

10

Teaching Juveniles

My next assignment would be to teach juvenile delinquents in a locked-down facility seventy-five miles from home. I am sure I could have been better prepared for this last job working in a prison. I began with a positive attitude, thinking that this was a calling that the LORD wanted me to embrace and the only open door to teaching full-time at my age (I told the LORD I wanted to return to teaching full-time in the public school system. I wasn't more specific than that).

Our church had a ministry day to highlight different ministry opportunities. I became interested in the prison ministry and talked with the minister in charge. It sounded exciting, and I knew Jesus told me to visit the prisons. I had yet to do that, so I signed up for the all-day workshop and the opportunity to minister in the county prison about thirty miles away. I volunteered to help once or twice a month for about a year. Then, I was given the opportunity to interview with two education programs working with juvenile delinquents. I asked a friend to pray with me for the right career choice and enhance my retirement. One took longer. Though it seemed like a better atmosphere, it was privately run. I am certain I chose the right one, but there were some doubts that first year!

I was hired in September, even though school started a month earlier. I asked to start in two weeks to de-stress from my last job and, also, because I had two weeks of vacation time saved.

Knowing I was already working, that sounded reasonable. (I had two weeks of vacation time saved). Meanwhile, SM planned to visit his daughter to help with his grandson for the next two weeks.

"I got the job! Do you mind if I go to the beach with the singles over Labor Day?" I asked.

"Sure, go and enjoy yourself," he assured me. (He had no control issues). It was a long trip to Ocean City alone (especially since I messed up the directions using the GPS in my excitement). Though it was a fun weekend, that's when I dropped my phone in the ocean. Lord knew I needed my phone as it was my only connection to relatives, work, and friends.

My job working with juvenile delinquents is detailed in the following two chapters. I am grateful that a student, GN, gave me a typed eight-page paper of his experience over the last three and a half years. If anyone was going to succeed, it was GN. He had a positive attitude, a good work ethic, and changed behavior. He took advantage of learning various certifications. He gave me permission to edit and use his paper as I told him I would write a book.

I was so thankful for a teaching job that I was willing to drive forty-five miles one way when gas prices were over $4.00 a gallon (I filled my tank twice a week). My previous job was very stressful, and now I would be getting paid $10,000 less than a starting teacher in my local school district, which was the only one contracted by a school district with no union. I was supposedly getting credit for six years of experience and a master's degree. I would have a free holiday and a month off in the summer, and the school year was an extra two weeks with pay. Truthfully, I wasn't working just for the money, although I was single the first year and living alone.

The first interview was held in a prison setting in the mountains, previously a hospital grounds for tuberculosis patients. Ours was a new facility away from other buildings, complete with a razor-wire enclosure around the building, including an outside area around the basketball court for each wing. I parked my car in the lot and walked one hundred feet to the entrance. A security guard recognized me and opened the first door. My bags could be randomly checked at any time. I was given a locked box to put my car keys and anything valuable that would fit. The guards would then open the next set of doors. This section housed the students in two large wings, one on each side. Each guy had a small room with a bed, a simple desk, a toilet, and a sink. A larger area with foldable tables was used to eat. When cleared, it became a basketball court—small offices in the far end for staff/ guards and counselors.

Beyond that was another set of doors the guards opened to the school. The school area was rather small compared to the students' living quarters. Perhaps as an after-thought, We need a school as these juveniles are under twenty-one. When you entered the educational wing, our faculty bathrooms and rooms for the secretary and principal's office were on the right side. There were seven classrooms: a smaller room for the counselor and another for the supply room with the aide's desk. Six rooms were set in a circular area around the seventh computer room across from a small kitchen area. Each space included an emergency exit that was also enclosed with razor wire. In fact, before the students left the van, they entered an enclosure area with razor wire. They went with shackles around their feet as an additional precaution. Seeing all these precautions might frighten a young teacher, but having volunteered in the county jail, a closed door didn't scare me. However, seeing a student being forced down by two larger guards and placed in shackles at the end of the day alerted me to the danger I faced daily.

"The students live here, so there are no snow days.

Are you okay with that drive?" the principal asked me.

"Sure," I assured him, remembering that black icy road one winter. I drove the back roads, enjoying the pastoral setting through the apple orchards rather than the interstate highway. I would surely be late if there were an accident on the highway. I trusted driving the less traveled roads. Later, the principal would be more lenient when road conditions were terrible. After a two-hour drive to school one snowy day, I decided to take "leave on a few nasty winter days." The science teacher had a long drive and never wanted to close school for inclement weather.

The students were divided into two sections, the Alpha and Charlie groups. The Charlie guys were the sex offenders. Typically, they had been abused by a relative or friend of the family, only to, in turn, violate someone else. It was a vicious cycle. Initially, I thought the Alpha guys were drug dealers, and some were. Their file usually read Aggressive behavior, which encompassed everything but sex offenders. However, if one large guy attacked a smaller guy, he would be moved to the Charlie area. Shortly before I left, I would be enlightened to learn that some of my students committed armed robbery, involuntary manslaughter, and other violent crimes. The less I knew at the beginning, the better I was.

I never had to deal with student problems with drugs or weapons, but that's not to say it wasn't dangerous. The guys used their bodies as weapons, and their anger could accelerate from one to one hundred within minutes. That's faster than you could call for help!

I had something in common with some of my students, as neither of us ate pork. I didn't because of a "nutritional kick" I learned in class years ago. They abstained because of Muslim tenets.

The first year was all about discipline, and having read the first few chapters, you know that was not my strongest area. Have strict rules and be consistent in enforcing them. Do not let them see any weakness or impartiality. Then I heard the story of the last English teacher who had been a security guard and, before that, a Marine. She gave JL a "U," which meant a negative six points on the discipline scale (and loss of a level in addition to losing the privilege of earning money for extras). Angrily, he returned to her room at lunchtime when the large door was not securely closed. He socked her right in the jaw. She hit her head on the corner of the wooden desk and suffered a concussion. She tried to return a bit later but couldn't function. I got the student's names mixed up as they all seemed odd. I gave preference to one student. It was not a good idea, as others would perceive I was weak and expect special treatment. They would test me again and again.

I got blamed for things I did or didn't do as I was the only female teacher, an easy scapegoat for all teachers. Until I got the students' respect, they also blamed me. Dusty swallowed a battery from the television remote just to get out of class. (What was he thinking?)

He could have died. He mentioned CH and my name. I got written up, but I still had my batteries. Thank God the student didn't die. And I cleared my name.

I put heavy colored tape around my desk and computer. "Do not go in this area," I would repeat repeatedly. I had to rearrange my classroom so that no one could hide behind a bookcase to do some evil deed and blame me! Just because they could. I was the responsible one! I prayed every day on the way to work, but it wasn't until I prayed over each desk and doorpost that I saw results. I enlisted a few others to pray for me as well. I survived that first year even though I was on probation for the first several quarters.

The following year, the governor required cameras in our classrooms. That ended my initiation, with no more blame for me. Very few co-workers were sure that I would survive. Now, the emphasis of teaching was individualization. I had several reading levels for vocabulary, study skills, reading books, and newspapers. I had all my tools, and they worked!

It was November 2 of my second year when my oldest son returned from Iraq—the very day we found out that Bryte had died. (I received the call on my way home from work). I was given five days of leave, but then they called to change it to three days, meaning I would need to return on Monday. I wasn't ready and used my leave for the extra day. The following work day, X came. His file said "Aggressive," but he was moved to the Charlie group at some point as a sex offender. In our morning meeting, I was advised not to accept his foul language, jokes, or misdeeds. Report any bad behavior. (This guy, X, was massive and reminded me of Frankenstein).

I confess I talked to God and said, "LORD, I don't understand how my son, who committed no crime, would die, but these criminals, who are a pieces of shit, are still living." There was no answer then or ever. (I had to surrender my need to know. I believe Bryte may have given up on life, though it was not ruled suicide, and there were no drugs involved. There was a cord above his bed and in the bathroom that he could have pulled at any time).

X didn't have a good attendance record, so the principal offered incentives for each day he stayed in school. He would play basketball with him, another student team, and a teacher. That seemed to work for several months.

I asked the security guards (staff) if someone would sit outside my room during that class period, but I was denied. Harvey, our eighty-plus-year-old aide, volunteered in my classroom during that period. I seated X up front next to the door. I positioned my chair close to him as I tutored him. I didn't have any books on that elementary level, so I had X dictate a story about his brother and family. I would write the story to read together, and then he would read it.

Meanwhile, he was "getting excited under his desk," which I was unaware of then. One day, he refused to work. Rather than wasting my time, I returned to work with another student. That's when he touched my back, or was it my backside? I asked him to go back to the computers and asked Harvey to watch my class. I then alerted the staff to have the principal look at the camera tapes. He did and told me I should watch them during my next free period (two hours after lunch). That was a long wait for something that important!

Previously, if I had said something to my students about my weekend (because they asked me) or anything outside the classroom, I was asked immediately to meet with the principal while Harvey babysat my class. Now I had to wait.

Watching the tape, I was convinced that X had crossed the line and touched me inappropriately. I pressed charges to send the rest of my students a message: "Don't mess with 'K!'" I never had to have this student in my classroom again. He may have sat with the counselor. I do not recall. That summer, V and X decided they'd rather go to the Big House (County Prison) with others who went last year. They found a piece of sheet metal and hit the supervisor over the head. Quickly, they got their wish!

After that first year, I greeted new students with a high kick with my right and left leg. With arms pointing in his face, I'd yell, "Don't mess with me!"

It became my trademark in the second, third, and fourth years!

Most of my students were from the Philadelphia area, but one was from Harrisburg, about ten miles from where I lived. His mom and sibling had all died in a fire while he was in prison. He was granted leave for the weekend with his aunt. But he didn't return to school in time, so he was AWOL (absent without leave). She overheard him talking about injuring someone while on the phone. She called the police. But while he was still missing, I had a bad dream and thought I heard him on my roof. As I got out of bed, I saw flashing red lights outside my window. I was sure he was after me. I was so upset I couldn't go to work the next day. Later, I found out my neighbor had a heart attack, and the red lights were the ambulance!

One day, near the end of the class period, I allowed Charlie's class to listen to music. One guy chose a country song, but R started to pound his head repeatedly on his desk—not once or twice but multiple times violently. I had to call out for the staff to take him out. He apologized after individual counseling and a brief meeting with the principal, me, and his counselor. He realized his inappropriate actions and was welcomed back to my classroom.

At the end of the school day, I gathered a work assignment to drop off at the Charlie Wing, where one of my students resided. I put his assignment on the table and saw "chocolate pudding on his window."

Only it wasn't chocolate pudding, but his feces. (I sure hope he had to clean it, but I think they got a giant hose to clean it).

Another time, I smelt "that foul odor" in a Charly guy's pants.

"He enjoys the squishy feel in his pants," I was told.

"Exit, please!" (I called the staff).

A new guy who wasn't very popular arrived, perhaps because he talked a lot. A few guys cornered him when he came out of the shower. They sucker-punched him and broke his jaw. The poor guy had to have his jaw wired. That meant he couldn't talk or eat. The kind nurse would make him a peanut butter smoothie. However, he couldn't brush his teeth either, and getting close to him was unpleasant due to the smell.

Students would ask Harvey, our aide, to help them get on the internet to research their senior project. (Probably they asked him because he was a "nice old man").

"Don't look," he said as he entered his password. But they did! Later, they would use it on the weekend to access the internet in their wing. They were caught chatting with college females and who knows what else. This happened twice. Consequence: A slap on the wrist the first time. The next time, he lost his privilege of using the teachers' computers in the classroom. He was still permitted to use his laptop in his corner of the supply room. (I am just sharing the inequality). He was a likable and dependable aide and substitute when we needed one. He always had my back when I required help. (Ten years later, I know he's not working there. Shortly after I left, he told me it was depressing for him at work. Few teachers cared).

Another incident in our other juvenile delinquent facility fifty miles away impacted me. Though I hadn't visited it, I understood it was less secure than our building. The students were permitted to go to other facilities within their complex. The other female reading teacher had an affair with a sixteen-year-old student. Someone found a note in her desk. Perhaps she was sick that day. It was meant for that particular male student: "I think I am pregnant." She had asked to tutor this young guy when he finished his math class. Then, they would have some "private time" in her closet.

All eyes were now on me, the only female teacher with an all-male student population! Wait, first, I have no interest; second, I have no closet; third, I am engaged; and fourth, my door is always open when students are in there! (This teacher had been a parole officer before getting her teaching degree. What was she thinking? She had a daughter the same age. And she lived in a small town where everyone knew her. She ruined her marriage, her family, her job, her pension, and her life). The student got scared and ran away rather than testify. That was the last I heard of that incident.

My students excelled and progressed in several grade levels. One improved four grade levels in reading in four months!

"What did I do? Tell me, what made the difference?" I asked.

"You," he answered, "you made me work and do a few more pages when I wanted to quit. And if I stayed longer, I would have improved even more."

He had a good attitude. He also improved in math and English, but not as drastic. The counselor gave a basic test when they entered our school and as they left to assess their progress (and probably access our school, too).

One of our youngest students was fourteen years old and had never been in a school setting. We were told that he was institutionalized for violent behavior, such as setting fires when he was young. There may be more to this story. The teachers would tutor him in the kitchen during our planning period to acclimate him to our school. I had to start from the beginning with the alphabet and its sounds. He progressed rapidly, and he was reading scientific books within two years!

In my last year, the five best students with good behavior and grades (of the Alpha group one semester and then the Charlie group) had an opportunity to enlist in the welding program. They were permitted to wear nice clothes and no shackles while traveling in the van or to the community room to take lessons. This was the best opportunity in four years as it gave the students hope for their future.

Before I left that fourth year, I was asked to share my curriculum in detail. After that first year, I was required to individualize my lessons. Some were bright *Scholastic* newspapers on various levels, and others were aimed at adults with remedial education on multiple levels. I compiled my curriculum instead of attending a two-day state conference with other teachers.

***

Things I Learned

From My Incarcerated Prison Students

1. Give me another chance to prove myself, whether I deserve it or not.

2. Respect me! I am human and know I made mistakes, but I am not a dog.

3. Show no favoritism. Treat all of us the same. We will test you. We do not respect the weak.

4. People lie: do not believe all of them, but believe me! (Wait a minute—didn't you just say not to show favoritism?).

5. Respect my religion and beliefs. Honor my dietary and holy days of fasting. I did have a question: doesn't your religion forbid drug and alcohol use? Yes, but we're not perfect. Their friends did drugs and had weapons. But they were good practicing Muslims. I am just repeating their words.

6. We will work harder or quicker for rewards. For the last five to seven minutes, I permitted music to be played on my computer for all to hear. Later, I was asked to initiate a contest to reward reading more books. I bought burgers, soda, and chips. I even read a book to verify it.

7. Grooming is believing they are honest and want to please you so you will trust and reward them. For example, a good student asked if he could clean my classroom as the teachers were left with that job. I verified the details and allowed him to work with supervision during my free period. He noticed a tote under my desk. "My mom says, "You shouldn't keep your purse on the floor." (He really wants to know if valuables are in the bag). "Oh, that's not my purse," I said as I showed him a book and some papers. He still asked for money for a soda. "Sorry," I replied truthfully. I don't bring money or valuables in here.

8. Teach me something I need to know. So, I made learning relevant and meaningful to them. I provided newspapers on various reading levels.

11

JV Student Writings

Troublesome

I first got locked up in '05 for shooting in school. Someone said I did it, but they had no evidence on me, so they sent me to Detention Center. I ran away when I was supposed to go to court. I turned myself in a month later. They put me on house arrest, but I cut it off as soon as I got in the house and went 'on the run' for a year straight.

Then, in '06 I got locked up for an attempted murder. I was sent to the county, but I was fighting it for 8 months. I beat the case because of a lack of evidence, and the witness didn't show up. I was home for a couple months. After that, I got locked up for a gun.

While I was fighting the case for 8 months, my

cousin got killed. He was real close to many, and that messed me up the most. They then sent me to Abraxas for two years. (A special school for juveniles).

Then I came home 2-9-09, but I missed my court date. Then I got shot up on 8-19-09. I was taken to the Youth Study Center for a warrant.

Then, they sent me to New Castle (a secure juvenile prison near Pittsburgh). I was to stay for 6-9 months, but they made me stay for a whole year. I came home 6-11-10.

Then the WORST thing happened to me when I thought everything was good: my little brother got killed on 7-11-10. Then I started to act a fool.

Then, my PO (parole officer) sent me to Vision Quest (an alternative program to detention to help previously incarcerated youth transition back into society in Pennsylvania) for 60 days. But then I got locked up a couple hours later for a shooting with two guns in a ski mask. Then, they gave me 2 to 4 years at SMSTU, but a week later, my lawyer got my case reopened. Then, I beat the shooting with one gun and was sent back to SMSTU for a year.

—BS

The Great Thing About Treatment

From the ages of 13-18 years old, I was very selfish, troubled, angry, and bad. I did things like drink, fight, smoke, and destroy property. I remember throwing up my meds, and I was very scared when I was angry.

But when I got locked up, I realized that if I ever wanted to feel peace inside and have a good life or as normal as possible, I needed to do something to change my ways. So, I accepted the fact that I needed treatment. So for four years, I took anger management, DBT group, sexual offending treatment, and how to use skills to control my anger.

I am not saying that I am entirely out of anger or perfect, but I am not that person anymore. I now have empathy for people, and I help people. I am a good person now. So, I hope you can take something from it and know you can change and feel peace. When you get help, it's a good thing, so don't feel ashamed about it.

—JJS

Graduation Speech

First, I want to thank (name of instructors). Since day one, our teachers were open and honest with us. They never judged nor belittled us. Our instructors motivated us and were devoted to helping us. I came into the welding program because of the money that I was told could be made.

About 4 months ago, I was asked if I was going to make a career out of it, and I said, "I don't think I can do this forever." Then, after reading the blueprints of my project, I actually understood the symbols, and I became very pleased with myself. Building my grill gave me a rush that made me feel good. Knowing that I can build something from the ground up gave me the love that I now have for welding.

Coming into the welding program, I was very nervous about being able to develop the skills needed to be successful in this field. One of the first questions R asked was, "Are you nervous?" I believe we all were, but R assured us that we'll all make it if we work hard for it and that no one would fail.

I thought to myself that this must be easy, or this lady must perform miracles. Not only did I gain welding skills, but I also learned that you have to work hard for what you want. Also, that nothing is given; you must strive for the best if that's what you possess.

There were days that I was tired of welding and days that Mr. D would come to me and say, “You can do this—it takes practice.” I feel like welding provided a sense of structure and discipline for me. It also taught me that you should never back down from a challenge, even when things become difficult. I learned to live by the saying, “Nothing is impossible, just difficult.”

Now that I completed welding everything that I come across, I seem to notice that it has been welded, and I could guess the type of weld it is. When I am welding in my booth, the only thing going through my mind is how beautiful I want this weld to turn out! But when it’s not to my satisfaction, I become very irritated, and at times I would take a walk.

During those times Mr. D would say, "What cha doing?" I would laugh and say, “I am done welding forever.” He would laugh as well and tell me to go in the booth so he can show me a different way to do it. And most of the time, it worked.

My staff played a major part as well. There were plenty of times that we were feeling down and times that I would become discouraged, and staff would remind us that all the hard work will pay off at the end. Look at us now; we stand as certified welders. Who would have ever thought that life would take us down this road?

We had a great support system, and I am truly appreciative of it. Because of this opportunity my life will never be the same. Not only did I do this for myself, most importantly, I did this for my son and the life that I can provide for him as well. This is an accomplishment that I know my mother and family will be proud of.

I want my son to be able to look into my eyes and see a hardworking man who provides for his family. And one day, I want to look into his eyes and see a man who works hard and provides for his family. Once again, I would like to thank everyone for the help that was given to me: to allow me to take my first step into a successful and healthy lifestyle.

—AT

My Point of View: Intake

That very moment you're on your way out of your city, hood… you take that last look of your environment and think of what you could've done better to avoid the day you got arrested or what you should've said to the individuals you were with when it all went down. But now it's too late; you're on your way to a lockdown facility for a long time, and the only thing you want to do is get it over with and go back to the block and family and move on. Do what you got to do to make it through without any issues.

You're now out of "your territory," and you don't know anybody, but you are ready and prepared for the unknown. One of the weirdest feelings in the world is when two guys stand there and watch you remove your clothing to check you for contraband. To me, that's like the top 5 of human violations against one another. You witness how some male staff start to puff their chest out and get big with you from the start. They attempt to put fear in your heart; that makes them look weird (not strong). That's a sign of what's to come here in the future.

Now you have this weird vibe going on because you see people all around you speaking and being polite, but you just got sentenced to a juvenile facility to do time. Being polite is the last thing on your mind. (So, not saying much to anybody is my way to go). Seeing other kids here in the hall, you think they are trying to show off and make themselves seem tough. They are just here to notice what brand of clothes you got locked up in and what city you're from. Meeting people upon intake sucks because you're tired and you're thinking about the amount of time you got.

Just hearing, "This is going to be your room," made me more mad than when I walked in the building. It's a little cell, not a room, designed to keep you locked in—until they're ready to let you out. Inside your cell, you got your sweatpants, sweatshirts, socks, t-shirts, school pants, boxers, shower slides, and a pair of cheap sneakers. All freedom is lost. Now, you are under the supervision of individuals who bleed the same blood as you, but they get paid to watch your every move. There is a handbook you are given to study to give you the gist of how things work here. The first three days of orientation, I didn't do anything but sleep and eat. That handbook wasn't important to me at the time.

The First Year

In the beginning, I just wanted to sleep and wake up and find out it's been a dream, but it wasn't. I was sitting in the TV section of the unit almost every day watching different staff come up to me. They'd tell me a little bit about themselves to make me feel better, but it didn't work. I found myself a part of a group after a few days playing spades, a card game with other residents on the unit. I was all right for the moment, playing basketball and just chilling on the unit every day. I didn't know my counselor yet, because she was on vacation when I arrived. When she returned and I met her, I knew 'we were going to be cool.'

As time moved on, there was some good staff, disrespectful staff, careless staff, and ignorant staff, but that's how the game of life goes. They all got their secrets. You got the ones who care and the ones who don't care at all. The entire facility was full, and things were fine. There was little drama from time to time. My family was coming up to see me. I was getting phone calls and talking to my counselor, and life locked up so far was "at a good pace." I had plans for going up the level system and doing well for my judge, counselor, 'the love of my life' and my family. There were days when people tried me, but I didn't let it get to me. I just looked at what I had and just laughed at them.

As I was going up the level system, I got more phone calls and more privileges. I wanted to work my way up to the highest level, Platinum, to start getting home passes. I learned later that I didn't need to reach that level for a pass. I just needed to ask the judge when I went to court. So, time went on, and I finally found myself wrapped up in a bit of trouble over a pill that no one knew what it was. Because I didn't report the unknown pill, I got my level dropped. By now, my birthday has passed. I am 18 years old, and I am working to make money for when I leave. I have a good relationship with a lot of residents now and a couple staff as well. I am in groups that are supposed to help me in the long-run in life after incarceration. Some of them are helpful, and some of them aren't. I only say that because I've been locked up so long and seeing so many of the kids who left this place are locked up again. It's sad because they try to teach educational groups in here, but truth is that the only thing going on in their heads is thinking of smarter ways to go back to the real world and 'trap' (sell drugs) without getting caught again.

Being an Honest Citizen

Since being locked up in here for so long, I've gotten in trouble a lot because I knew about things, but I didn't report them, nor did I open up and say: "Listen, this has been going on for a while." As a result, I got penalized.

I know that in here, they preach that being honest and doing the right thing is always the way to go, but I highly disagree. Where I am from I was raised to believe that sometimes 'if it doesn't involve you or your family, that you should mind your own business.' I know there are people out there that don't agree with me at all, and that's cool.

But I will never put myself in a position to report somebody that can come back to me or my family in the long run (that's in jail or out of jail). In my world, if you know something and report XYZ, then days, weeks, months, or even years go by, and that same XYZ or somebody connected to that individual comes around to hurt you and your family.

I am an honest person, but depending on what the situation is and who's involved, I am going to live my life and not worry about anyone else. Especially if it doesn't affect me in any way.

The Second Year

This is when I considered myself officially part of this place. I reached platinum level. I got a good relationship with most of the staff, my probation officer, and my judge who approved me to go off-grounds outside the facility. I felt like "Time is on a roll." At this point in time, things are comfortable where I am at now. So, they can show their true colors to be disrespectful and use their power to make me feel down. But I don't fall for it: I just "let it go." Well, I guess you can say I am getting smart and not falling for it!

Around this time, I notice that I am in too deep with the kids here, and I know things that I don't want to. But at the end of the day, it's none of my business what they got going on. I experienced residents getting a hold of things they shouldn't have from other staff. During this time, I think I witnessed a series of relationship-building between residents and staff. I saw how new people got hired, and old people still did the usual things. My biggest question was: "Do they really know who they are hiring?" Some staff can stand their ground and know that this is their job. They know what's right and what's not. You got staff who want to be welcomed by the residents, so that's when kids "go in for the kill." They talk them into getting things that they shouldn't have and could get them fired.

Going off-grounds was fun as I enjoyed spending time away from that building and some people. I was able to clear my mind and have fun. I had a crazy relationship with a lot of staff at this point. I was making money working jobs and was on my way to getting home passes. Things were good. There were days I wish I was in real prison and not here because of the way I was getting treated, my surroundings, and things that happened back home while I was here. In the middle of the year: while I was waiting to get a phone call to talk to my family, I found out my cousin was killed. After hearing that, I didn't know what to do. I felt stuck. I just wanted to break down and destroy everything, but I knew that wouldn't get me anywhere. I didn't want to tell anyone when I heard the news. I waited for a little while to open up and express it. That was 'my boy.' We did almost everything together. We were in the same class in school, rode the same bus, lived 2 minutes away, and hung out just about every day. The night he was killed, they were just hanging out in front of his mom's house. Some random guy from across the street just started firing his gun into the crowd. They all ran for cover, but my cousin got shot in the back a couple of times. They carried him into the house, and he died on his mom's couch only thirty days after his eighteenth birthday.

Three days after I got the bad news about my cousin, I called home again to see how everyone was doing. This time, my sister told me that my long-time neighbor, who knew me since I was 7 years old, died from diabetes. He was 27 years old. And a day later, another friend of mine got into a real bad four-wheeler accident and was badly injured. That was the worst week ever, as everyone who had been around me had died or got hurt. If I wasn't here, I would have been with one of them. That could have happened to me. I honestly believe that was a major loss and change for me. Knowing when I eventually returned home, they wouldn't be around.

At the end of summer, another birthday passed; I was 19 years old. I was moved off my unit to another unit, which made me mad. No one cared the entire time. Instead, they kept preaching to me that in the real world I am going to have to deal with change and that I have an issue accepting change. I tried to explain to them that putting me in a group of negative guys when I was on the highest level and doing good didn't make sense. It wasn't right, but I had no choice. I had to let it go and deal with it.

Change. To me being locked up means that "life was put on hold," as I am on the inside, and whatever goes on in the outside world I have no control over anymore because I am not available.

I am still locked up and away from family and friends. It's been a BIG change. Life is different in here. I am surrounded by authority, and all my rights are gone. I was moved to a unit full of negativity, and it wasn't positive, nor realistic. (It's like forcing an honor student to be in a class full of negative kids who don't care about their education. They do drugs after school, and then that honor student becomes part of that crowd to do drugs and eventually drop out of school). Here, you cannot express yourself and come up with a game plan.

Dealing with the loss of my family was the BIG change for me. I didn't need another change.

The Third Year

I almost lost my Platinum level, as I didn't care anymore. Motivation from my counselor, probation officer, my family, and my judge turned me around so I kept going. By now, I've been on about 5 home passes. Things at home were good: the family and same city. It felt so good to be home, but the worse part was going back. The place was hiring new staff, and things weren't the same any more. A lot of kids left, and now I am still here where I started having to make new friends again. I tried to get an early release in court, but that was denied. Nothing major: I just had to serve my time. By now, I was moved from unit to unit until I stopped complaining. No one was listening, and it was my word against theirs. Nine out of ten times you lose and they win (that's one percent that's left. You need to "walk with angels" to win a battle against authority).

I am getting close to my 20th birthday, and I feel more mature than the last time I was home at 16. In my mind, the whole teenager thing "is out the window," but some staff didn't believe that. I've been disrespected and criticized in here. But I have always believed in Karma: things may not always come back to that individual but to someone close to that individual. Another thing I learned: "Treat others the way you want to be treated." Cause what goes around comes around.

To survive, I set goals for myself and put my family first and "rolled with it." Being locked up since I was 16 years old, I'd say the biggest change was from maturity. Being surrounded by good people and building a positive relationship in places is key to changing. My counselor, probation officers, the clerk typist, TSC, my PSA, youth advocate, learning center, work training coordinators, program manager, maintenance repairman, nurse, and some of the youth development aids assisted me. I appreciated each of them for helping me and taking the time to talk to me and give me positive reinforcement.

It's my last year, and the countdown is on. Now I feel like everything I worked for is about to hit me real soon. It's been 4 years, 7 months since I've been free. Knowing my time is near is a wild feeling: just to enter the real world again and be free again. The days start to get a little longer. Word spreads that I am the next up to leave. Others try to bring me down, while others are happy to see you succeed and others don't care at all.

Now I am down to 29 days of my journey locked up in a juvenile facility. I appreciate the good things in life and the good people I have met that have had an impact on my life. I won't make the decision that got me into trouble in the past. Now I've made the smart decision to get through with being incarcerated and take my second chance at life and run with it in a positive way.

I've been given the opportunity to have a home pass every month, attend online college classes, and assist in community service projects off-grounds and get seven certifications (Forklift, OSHA, ServSafe, CPR, Commit to Clean, First Aid ICDL). That will help me get a better job as well as graduate and get a diploma.

The duration of my stay here at SMSTU helped me grow and change the way I think, cope and react better in life. One thing I learned and realized in placement was that you are never entitled to anything. Things you want in life you must work for and commit to your goals. By creating a positive game plan and taking one day at a time helped me stay focused on reaching my goals. I choose to live a positive, crime-free life. Over the past 3 years, I've met people that I don't want to let down. Instead, I want to call in the future to let them know how good life is on the outside.

My overall experience in placement was life-changing. I am changed in the way I see things in life, the way I interact with people, and I choose not to judge. (Being locked up, some people judge others too much. They don't understand that people make mistakes but they can change). Everything in life is a choice and I choose to live my life and not destroy it.

—GN

Epilogue

It's a Wonderful Life!

If you have gotten this far, reader, I hope you can see how my life is a testament to God's love. Through the hardships of a troubled childhood, the loss of my middle son, and the end of my first marriage after four decades, I can testify that the foundation that has held me up over all these years is the simple truth that God loves me.

Not only has God's love kept me, but it has also allowed me to find love again. I married my husband, Santiago, on July 22, 2012, and retired in June 2014. For people in our twilight years, you would think we would be slowing down—but we're not! My husband loves to travel and has taken me on more adventures in eleven-and-a-half years of marriage than I experienced in my first fifty years! To share how God has helped to heal the wounded parts of me through travel, I want to share with you some of my travel highlights:

2012—Puerto Rico. Kayaked in Bioluminescent Bay, where we saw iridescent fish in the waters. We ate a kabob as well while wading in the water at Luquillo Beach.

2012—Costa Rica. Toured the hot springs, where we took the fast slide into the water (Santiago went under and had to be rescued). Ziplined for the first (and last!) time. Saw more animals on this trip than anywhere else.

2013—Nova Scotia, Canada. Enjoyed local music and a local clogging dance in Nova Scotia.Beautiful landscapes. Great food.

2014—New Zealand. Took a relaxing mud bath in New Zealand, a boat ride in Waitomo Caves (with glow worms), an evening of cultural dance (we joined the dance group on stage), and dinner (cooked underground). Toured the North Island with a couple we hosted two years prior. Participated in a bird show and milked a cow at an agriculture show. Visited a local school and a modern dairy farm.

2014—Australia. Flew from New Zealand to Australia, where we saw a double rainbow in the sky! On our first full day, we saw a koala relaxing in a tree in the wild, kangaroos, various birds, and other wildlife. Toured classes in local schools and attended a reception by local government officials. Walked the Otway Fly Tree Top. Saw the Twelve Apostles (a collection of limestone stacks located in the Port Campbell National Park, Victoria, Australia).

Stayed with two different families, spending the last few days in Melbourne.

2015—Spain & Portugal. Left $100 worth of souvenirs on the bus on this trip. Ate grilled sardines. I bought a purse made of cork (I still have that one). A fish in the aquarium nibbled on my feet!). Beautiful architecture, cathedrals, and the largest serpentine beach in the world.

2016—Italy & Gibraltar. Saw the Vatican and rode the Amalfi Coast. Also, rode a gondola. We saw many beautiful murals, cathedrals, and architecture from coast to coast.

2017—Panama Canal, Panama, Costa Rica, and Small Islands Cruise. Snorkeled and was quarantined in my room for a few days due to a stomach bug while three guys in masks cleaned my room.

2017—England. Traveled with Friendship Force (our travel group). Saw where *Poldark* and *Downton Abbey* were filmed. Ate lunch at Lanhydrock, a Victorian Country house that looked like a giant castle (where the owners lived on the upper floor).

2018—China. Saw pretty much everything except the Panda Bears (Sichuan Province). Saw Tiananmen Square, the Terracotta Warriors, and walked the Great Wall. Saw silkworms making silk. Got fingerprinted and had eye recognition technology used on me at the airport. Watched live shows, took boat rides, and had Happy Birthday! Sung to me.

2018—Israel. Visited with a local church the sites where Jesus walked. I joined our group to spend an hour or so cleaning the beach (The "Beautiful Land Initiative"). I bought a tee shirt to help with expenses. Floated in the Dead Sea (I got stuck in the mud!), took Communion in the Garden of Gethsemane, climbed the Israel fortress at the Golan Heights, took a boat ride on the Sea of Galilee. Visited a kibbutz where Israelis and Muslims worked side by side. Worshiped and sang songs. Saw many beautiful historic sites from the Bible.

2019—Peru, Machu Picchu, Ecuador, and Galapagos Islands. Skydived (with a guide) over Love Park. Took a train ride to Machu Picchu and walked the terraces. Visited a local farmers market to purchase food for dinner with a Peruvian family. Helped prepare the sides for the meal and ate with them. Took a tour of the local cemetery and learned of their customs.

2019-2022—We moved. COVID. Stateside tours.

2023—Grand Canyon, Arizona. Toured the Grand Canyon in a helicopter. Stayed on an Indian Reservation at Canyon De Shay, then toured the canyon in an old Army truck across the canyon floor. Took a pink Jeep tour up the mountains.

2023—Colorado. Toured Pikes Peak and visited Pagosa Hot Springs for three days.

I share these travel experiences for two reasons. First, who would have thought that someone like me would have a chance to travel the world this "late" in life? Second, God used many of my activities while traveling to help heal parts of me. So, I want to encourage you to look at the opportunities in your life, to dream, and to think positively.

- Instead of asking, *Why me?* say, *Thank you, God.*
- Look for the healing in the opportunity. If the opportunity is for you to be quiet and

alone, take that time to talk to God. If the opportunity is for you to be among your loved ones or friends, be grateful to the people around you who loved you.

My past is part of my sacred journey because it has made me who I am today. I might not have always followed God's perfect path, but He's been with me to guide me when I ask in faith. He's been able to make something good out of many bad situations.

While going through tough times, I have grown stronger, determined, and steadfast in my faith. Although there were times of despair and depression, prayers of friends brought me back.

I've learned to claim God's promise, claim His word, and pray more fervently. I have more empathy toward the suffering of others. I'm learning to be more thankful. I have hope for today and for the future when my sons can understand my past and forgive their mom of her shortcomings. To see the new me who has grown in love, in a new desire to be a bigger part of their lives and the lives of my granddaughters.

I have learned to see my weaknesses and appreciate how the Lord has made my journey a testimony of His unfailing love, mercy, and grace. He has redeemed my weak areas, making me able to sympathize and empathize with others in need. I've learned to accept my past and appreciate my journey so that I can move toward a better future.

But in fact God has placed the parts
in the body, every one of them
just as he wanted them to be.

I CORINTHIANS 12:18

The righteous will flourish like a palm tree,
they will grow like a cedar of Lebanon; planted in
the house of the Lord, they will flourish in the courts of
our God. They will still bear fruit in old age,
they will stay fresh and green,

PSALM 92:12-14 (NIV)

ACKNOWLEDGMENTS

To Eli Bortz, my editor, for his expertise and encouragement.

To my publisher for his creativity, expertise, and insight in recreating my life story.

To the following people and organizations: Tess and Pete Hamel; One Heart Ministries; www.wkbo.net for counseling, words of wisdom, encouragement, and prayers.

To my friends, family, and leaders who prayed for and encouraged me along the way. Your names are too numerous to count, lest I forget to mention someone.

Book Club

Reflection Questions

20 Questions

for Processing Child Abuse

1. Do I have difficulty trusting others due to my childhood experiences?

2. Have I developed coping mechanisms to deal with past trauma?

3. In what ways has childhood abuse impacted my self-esteem?

4. How did my caregiver's actions affect my sense of safety and security?

5. What impact has the abuse had on my mental and emotional well-being?

6. How do I view authority figures, and how does this relate to my past experiences?

7. Have I noticed any recurring nightmares or flashbacks related to my childhood?

8. What role has forgiveness played in my healing process, if at all?

9. How has my upbringing affected my parenting style, if applicable?

10. Do I struggle with feelings of guilt or responsibility for the abuse?

11. How have my past experiences influenced substance use?

12. How has my past shaped my perception of love and affection?

13. Have I developed maladaptive coping mechanisms to deal with stress?

14. How do I handle conflict, and has this been influenced by my childhood experiences?

15. How has my career or professional life been affected by my past experiences?

16. How do I feel about the concept of forgiveness for myself and others?

17. How have my experiences of abuse shaped my identity?

18. How do I navigate feelings of anger and resentment related to my past?

19. How do I approach self-care, and do I prioritize my well-being?

20. What would I say to my younger self, knowing what I know now about healing from childhood abuse?

20 Questions
for Processing Grief

1. What emotions are you experiencing right now?

2. Are there specific memories that bring comfort or pain?

3. What support systems have been most helpful for you?

4. How has your understanding of death evolved through this experience?

5. What rituals or practices bring you a sense of connection with the person you lost?

6. Have you found solace in creative outlets, such as writing or art?

7. How has your relationship with others changed since the loss?

8. What aspects of your loved one's legacy do you want to carry forward?

9. Are there unresolved issues or conversations that you wish you had with the person who passed away?

10. Have you experienced any physical symptoms of grief, such as changes in appetite or sleep patterns?

11. What role does spirituality or faith play in your grieving process?

12. Have you discovered new strengths or coping mechanisms during this time?

13. What self-care practices have been most effective for you?

14. How do you handle triggers that bring back memories of the person you lost?

15. Have you considered seeking professional support, such as counseling or therapy?

16. Have you found comfort in connecting with others who have experienced similar losses?

17. What role does forgiveness play in your healing process?

18. In what ways have your priorities shifted since the loss?

19. Have you experienced any dreams or significant symbols related to the loss?

20. What do you wish others understood about your grief?

20 Questions
for Processing Divorce

Divorce is a complex and emotional process, so use these questions to encourage reflection and self-discovery:

1. How are you feeling about the divorce right now?
2. In what ways has your self-perception changed since the divorce?

3. What support systems have been most helpful for you during this time?

4. Have you identified any patterns or behaviors within the marriage that you want to avoid in the future?

5. How do you navigate shared social circles and mutual friends post-divorce?

6. What self-care practices have been most effective in helping you cope with the emotional toll?

7. What role does forgiveness play in your healing process?

8. How do you navigate the dating scene or the prospect of forming new relationships?

9. What lessons have you learned about yourself through the divorce process?

10. Have you found comfort in connecting with others who have experienced similar divorces?

11. In what ways have your priorities shifted since the end of the marriage?

12. How do you handle moments of guilt or self-blame related to the divorce?

13. How do you celebrate personal growth and resilience in the face of divorce?

14. What advice would you give to others currently going through a divorce?

15. Have you considered creating a new vision for your future, independent of the past?

16. How do you balance the need for alone time with the importance of social support?

17. What strengths or qualities have you discovered within yourself that you didn't realize you had?

18. What aspects of your values or priorities do you want to prioritize moving forward?

19. How do you form new connections and relationships after a divorce?

20. What are your hopes and aspirations for the next chapter of your life?

20 Questions

for Processing Mental Illness

1. How are you feeling about your loved one's mental health right now?

2. What emotions arise when you think about their struggles?

3. How has your loved one's mental illness im-

pacted your daily life?

4. What are some challenges you face in supporting your loved one's mental health?

5. Are there specific aspects of their mental illness that you find particularly difficult to understand?

6. How has your relationship with your loved one changed since the onset of their mental illness?

7. How can I best support you as you help your loved one?

8. How do you handle frustration or helplessness in this situation?

9. What self-care practices have been most beneficial for you during challenging times?

10. How do you balance offering support and respecting their independence?

11. Have you considered seeking professional advice or counseling for yourself?

12. What do you wish others understood about the challenges you face in supporting someone with mental illness?

13, How do you handle moments of crisis or emergency related to your loved one's mental health?

14. Have you experienced challenges advocating for your loved one within the healthcare system?

15. How do you navigate conversations about treatment options and therapy with your loved one?

16. How do you handle situations where your loved one may resist or refuse help?

17. How do you navigate feelings of isolation or loneliness arising from this experience?

18. Have you found any strategies for managing the impact of your loved one's mental illness on your mental health?

19. How do you celebrate small victories and moments of progress in your loved one's mental health journey?

20. What are your hopes and aspirations for your loved one's future mental health, and how do you envision your role in that journey?

About the Author

Embark on a riveting journey through Karen's tumultuous life, where resilience and faith intersect. In this compelling narrative, humor and determination collide, painting a vivid picture of Karen's experiences filled with laughter, heartache, and an unshakable belief in the Divine. From the shadows of childhood abuse to the pinnacle of academic achievements, from passionate community activism to the depths of devastating loss, Karen's life unfolds as a whirlwind of unexpected adventure where the sky is the limit. Everyone Needs (Just a Little) Karen transcends the conventional memoir, emerging as a poignant and thought-provoking tale of a child's journey toward redemption and resilience in the face of life's formidable challenges.

Brace yourself for both giggles and tears as Karen lays bare her life, sharing the effects of childhood trauma, the uproarious blunders of growing up, and the poignant struggles of pursuing a career while raising a family. From the importance of speaking up for oneself to the comedic mishaps of everyday life, this little book offers a refreshing perspective on dealing with challenging situations and personalities in characteristically "un-Karenesque" ways.

With a touch of humor and empathy, Everyone Needs (Just a Little) Karen is an entertaining read that will leave you both chuckling and reflecting on the absurdities and essential life lessons hidden within those potentially "Karen" moments we all encounter. Discover in Karen's book the remarkable resilience of laughter, showing that even amid life's trials, laughter and grins can propel us forward.

GRIEF SHARE®

A support group to help you move through the grief process. Helping people find comfort after the loss of a loved one for 25 years.

www.griefshare.org

NAMI

National Alliance on Mental Illness

NAMI is the nation's largest grassroots mental health organization dedicated to building better lives for the millions of Americans affected by mental illness.

www.nami.org

The people of Kairos are called by God to share the love of Christ with those impacted by incarceration.

Traitmarker Media
www.traitmarkeremedia.com
traitmarker@gmail.com

Milton Keynes UK
Ingram Content Group UK Ltd.
UKHW041058010224
437093UK00004B/39

9 798869 004406